W9-CIQ-493

The Church Plans for
Kindergarten Children

This is one of a series of books produced for interdenominational use by the Protestant denominations working through the Cooperative Publication Association.

The Church Plans for Kindergarten Children

by
Kathrene McLandress Tobey

Published for
Cooperative Publication Association
by
THE WESTMINSTER PRESS
· PHILADELPHIA

UNITY SCHOOL LIBRARY
Unity Village
DISCARD
Lee's Summit, Missouri 64063

© W. L. JENKINS MCMLIX

All rights reserved — no part of this book may be
reproduced in any form without permission in
writing from the publisher, except by a reviewer
who wishes to quote brief passages in connection
with a review in magazine or newspaper.

Unless otherwise indicated, the Scripture quota-
tions are from the Revised Standard Version of
THE HOLY BIBLE, copyrighted 1946 and 1952
by the Division of Christian Education of the National Council of Churches, and used by permission.

LIBRARY OF CONGRESS CATALOG CARD No. 59–13436

PRINTED IN THE UNITED STATES OF AMERICA

Contents

THUS A CHILD LEARNS

Thus a child learns; by wiggling skills
through his fingers and toes into himself;
by soaking up habits and attitudes of
those around him; by pushing and pulling
his own world.

Thus a child learns; more through trial
than error, more through pleasure than
pain, more through experience than
suggestion, more through suggestion
than direction.

Thus a child learns; through affection,
through love, through patience, through
understanding, through belonging,
through doing, through being.

Day by day the child comes to know a
little bit of what you know; to think a
little bit of what you think; to understand your understanding. That which
you dream and believe and are, in truth,
becomes the child.

As you perceive dully or clearly; as you
think fuzzily or sharply; as you believe
foolishly or wisely; as you dream drably
or goldenly; as you bear false witness or
tell the truth — thus a child learns.

— Frederick J. Moffitt

Chapter 1

KINDERGARTEN CHILDREN ARE GROWING PERSONS

What will he be? We look at Warren, a four-year-old, on his first day in the church kindergarten. Here he stands surveying the room with questioning eyes. He may be holding back from this new experience; he may be eager and ready to get busy. His small, plump body betrays his nearness to babyhood. His short haircut and jaunty stance portray his manhood. We cannot help but wonder: What will he be like when he is grown? Will he be a plumber, a doctor, or a businessman? Will he attend church on Sundays or will he go fishing? Will he be trustworthy or just a little deceitful? Will he be selfish or have a genuine concern for others? What will determine his everyday choices — desire for things, desire for power, love of self, love of God?

The child Warren is today will condition the man he becomes tomorrow, just as the adult you are today depends in large part on the child you have been. Warren's parents have been his primary source of influence, but gradually teachers will also guide him. In nursery school and kindergarten he will find himself in a variety of situations in which he will make choices and weigh values in satisfaction or dissatisfaction. For his sake, it is beneficial if his parents and teachers become a partnership in which each helps the other to understand and meet his needs. It is also helpful if both have the same point of view in dealing with children. Some adults look upon a child as an empty house to be furnished with what they know; they do much talking in order to fill him with directions and information. Others look upon a child as a storehouse of innate abilities to be discovered and developed. This second point of view is, on the whole, the accepted one today. But even in giving directions and information, it is possible for adults to help the child understand himself and his world as they move through experiences with him. The best way to help children learn is through guiding them in making choices and in discovering meanings and values for themselves.

DETERMINING FACTORS IN CHRISTIAN NURTURE

Christian parents, teachers, and leaders look upon a child as another member of God's family in whom he has placed great potential and for whom he holds great hope. We share God's concern and offer ourselves as his instruments in helping the child grow to that fullness of which he is capable. We are aware of several great truths that are determining factors in our common task of Christian nurture:

Every person is important in the sight of God.

No two persons are identical; each has his own individuality.

All persons have similarities, particularly noticeable within a given age group.

All persons are constantly changing, growing.

All persons need one another in the process of learning and growing.

By his every word and deed Jesus pointed up the peculiar worth of each individual. As we mature, his life and teachings help us realize this in fuller measure, so that we come to cherish a person for himself, for his special combination of abilities and personality. So too a child must be accepted and respected as he is and loved and guided toward all that he is capable of becoming.

Secondly, it is an amazing fact that of all the millions of people on the earth no two are identical. Differences in physical stature and mental alertness are more readily seen than those that emerge in emotions and attitudes and personal relationships. Hardest to see are differences in the way each person grows — sometimes slowly, sometimes speedily; sometimes smoothly, often spasmodically. Therefore, it is evident that when a group of children come together, they cannot all be ready at a certain hour on a certain morning to learn the same thing. Their needs must be respected and their choices of activity encouraged.

Thirdly, along with being unique, human beings do have similarities. We are born as helpless babies in the same way, and we all grow through the same functional sequences. For example, we squirm before we crawl, we crawl before we toddle, we toddle before we walk, we walk before we run. The process is the same for all people in every country, even though the adults concerned may guide the baby differently. " We do not oppose nature; we cannot, at least, with any hope of success. As we learn more about the sequence of development, we can so arrange the environment as to prepare the child for next stages, but we cannot eliminate or alter the major steps in that sequence or change

to any significant degree the timing of that sequence." [1]
Recognition of our similarities as well as our differences
is basic to a Christian acceptance of God's laws of
growth.

Fourthly, human beings constantly grow or change. A
baby reacts to everything and everyone in its environment; he seeks to know the world around him. He
learns to like certain things and repeat them; he also
learns to dislike certain things and rebel against them.
His behavior indicates whether the learning at the moment is difficult or easy by the fact that he is hesitant
or adventurous, sad or happy, tense or at ease. Because
growth takes place continually, leaders of children must
be aware that children will learn both the good and the
bad, the expected and the unexpected. Within a child,
growing takes time; it cannot be hurried. To the adult
guiding a child, growing gives time; its opportunities
must not be overlooked.

Fifthly, individuals cannot be human beings alone;
they need one another. God plans for babies to be born
into families. Children need adults. In fact, all ages
need one another, for we learn and grow through our
relationships, our interdependence. For Christians, the
pattern of this life together has been set by Jesus; we
learn from him how to live in love as children of one
Father.

These five truths are determining factors in our task
of Christian nurture. They influence our attitudes toward our kindergarten children, what we teach them in
church and home, how and where we teach, and the
way in which the adults concerned work together.

[1] From *Child Development,* by William E. Martin and Celia Burns
Stendler. Used by permission of Harcourt, Brace and Company, Inc.,
publishers.

With this point of view let us turn to look at children who are four and five years of age. They continually surprise us, for they are changing rapidly. Often they bewilder us. But they need not baffle us completely, for we can study what they are like in general within each sequence of growth, and we can get acquainted with many of them personally. Then we will be alert both to their similarities or group ways of growing and to their individual patterns of growing.

What are children like at age four? That is, what are they becoming? Some may have three-year-old characteristics because of a slow rate of growth in particular areas, because of a prolonged illness, or because of being waited upon too much in a household of adults. Some may take on characteristics that seem to belong to five-year-olds because of a faster pattern of growth in particular areas, or because they live with older children or adults who play and read and talk with them. For the most part, however, we can see a fairly standard picture of their capabilities. Think of a four-year-old you know, as you study each characteristic. Then consider the "need" implied by that characteristic. This knowledge is fundamental to any guidance parents and teachers may give children.

THE FOUR-YEAR-OLD

His body

He is very active and growing rapidly. Therefore he needs

— freedom to skip, run, jump, walk, climb, hop.
— frequent changes of position, for he cannot sit still comfortably for more than five minutes.

He can control his arm, body, and leg muscles much better than his hands and feet. So he needs

— large materials for work and play: large lumps of clay, large crayons and brushes, large sheets of paper (at least 12″ x 18″), large blocks, and room for wide motions.

He tumbles and twirls for sheer pleasure. Therefore, it is good for him to have

— music suitable for all kinds of rhythmic motions.

When he is overactive and irritable, he may be fatigued or getting sick. He needs

— adults who notice and understand his trouble.

— a place to get away from people where it is quiet, with no sense of this being "punishment."

His mind

He can make decisions. Therefore he needs

— time for deciding which socks he will wear or which book he wants read.

— adults who are patient and encourage him to decide, whenever possible, rather than deciding for him to "save time."

He can think things through by himself or in a group. So he needs

— experiences in which he can plan and explain why he wants to do something a certain way.

— group experiences in which he can evaluate what has been done.

He is developing a longer attention span. He needs

— opportunities to choose what creative activity he will try.

— interesting materials to work with.

— casual encouragement in a continuing interest

He can carry out simple commands. So he needs

— adults who get his attention before giving a command.

— adults who can give clear, simple directions and are willing to repeat them for clarity.

— adults who show that they expect the request to be carried out and express their appreciation when it is done.

He has a vivid imagination and can pretend well. He needs

— adults who will read to him often.

— creative materials to work with, such as clay, paint, blocks.

— the joy of dramatic play.

— dress-up clothes and objects that will help him play the adult life he sees around him, such as being Daddy, Mother, the doctor, the mailman.

He talks a lot — not always because he has anything important to tell or ask, but to seek attention and friendliness. Therefore he needs

— adults who enjoy conversations with him.

He does not understand money values. So he needs

— opportunities to be helpful to others through what he can do and make for them rather than through the giving of money.

His Relationship with Others

He still enjoys being independent but begins to seek the companionship of other children. He needs

— opportunities during the kindergarten session to play and work with one or two at a time rather than with the entire group.

When he is with one or two compatible friends, he will exclude others from this group. He needs

— time to work and play with friends without interruption and directions from adults. At the same time, he needs helpful guidance in shifting such groups to include others.

He has a strong feeling for home and family. Therefore it is important that he

— have a share in the planning and carrying out of family affairs, such as trips, picnics, excursions, vacations, as well as the everyday routines of the home.

He talks freely about what happens at home. So he needs

— tactful parents who do not discuss everything in his hearing.

— tactful teachers who do not repeat what they hear the children say about home affairs.

He talks " big " — brags, boasts, threatens. He is not as brave inwardly as he sounds but is feeling his powers and trying them out. He needs

— sensitive, understanding adults who ignore such talk, join in humorously, raise questions gently.

He wants to be liked by adults and often seeks attention by showing off. So he needs

— adults who give him attention and love just as they give it to each and every child in the group or family.

— adults who encourage his work and efforts at better relationships and express their praise before he has to ask for it by his behavior.

He is not concerned with race, color, or religion. He accepts all children and adults as people. Therefore, it is essential that he have

— adults around him who are free from prejudice, hatred, and suspicion.

— adults who are sure that all people are children of God and who act and speak accordingly.

Some four-year-olds still resist authority by withdrawal

from the group, by hitting, pushing, and saying " I won't." They need

— adults who realize they are just growing out of three-year-oldness and find it difficult to do what they really want to do.

— help in learning acceptable ways of acting — often simple rules will guide them — so they will be liked and wanted by the group or family.

His feelings

He is often jealous, particularly of brothers and sisters. Therefore he needs

— adults who express their love of him and make him feel wanted and needed.

He is quarrelsome; he fights and cries. He needs

— help in solving the problems that cause his anger.

He is fearful. So he needs

— adults who will talk about the fear with him and help him understand what caused the fear.

He is loving. He needs

— to show his love and to be loved.

He is joyous about little everyday things that seem important and special to him. Therefore he needs

— adults who share his happiness and join in merrily.

If you teach four-year-olds only, then you have just read a brief, general description of your children. In order to really help them, you will want to know something of where they are going and what they will become when they are five years of age. The following chart will guide you in this. But if you teach only five-year-olds, you will need to know where they have come from. So study both charts, noting the differences in them and the progression in growth. Keep reminding yourself that these charts indicate stages or sequences of growth that *usually* take place during these years. They do not come at exactly the same time for every child, with the same intensity, or with the same speed of development. Therefore they are not exact descriptions but a guide in our effort to understand children.

Five-year-olds have arrived at a special stage of growing. They are poised and controlled, skillful in using many toys and work materials, adept at climbing, riding tricycles and scooters. They are happy and sure of themselves. All of this may not seem true to you on first glance, but if you know a five-year-old well, you can see that in the brief span of his lifetime, he has reached at this point a comfortable age. A growing person of five years of age has stopped to relax awhile, to enjoy life. For as he approaches his sixth birthday, he inevitably starts another difficult period of growth, and life is more strenuous. Psychologists tell us that we all went through such stable periods at about the ages of sixteen weeks, twenty-eight weeks, three years, five years, and ten years. These ages or periods were like plateaus in a long, steep mountain we were climbing. On the plateaus we breathed more easily and were less tense; it was the climbing that was difficult.

THE FIVE-YEAR-OLD

His body

He can wash, feed, dress, and toilet himself. He needs
  — adults who let him do things for himself and praise him for his accomplishments.

He is very susceptible to contagious diseases. He must be protected by

— adults who are consistent in helping him develop good health habits, such as using a handkerchief, washing hands, keeping things out of his mouth, taking drinks of water, and staying away from groups when not feeling well.

He has good control of arms and legs. Therefore he needs

— activities that will strengthen these large muscles — running, jumping, skipping, dancing, climbing, using tricycles, wagons, and large balls.

He has only fair control of the small muscles of hands and feet. So he needs

— large tools and materials for work and play, such as large brushes for painting, large crayons, sheets of paper at least 12″ x 18″, large lumps of clay, and puzzles with large pieces.

He is noisy and active, with a sense of purpose in his activity. So he should have

— work and play materials suited to his age and made available for his own choosing of what he will do — a scooter to manipulate, a truck to drive, a train to direct, a plane to pilot, salt dough to knead, and a baby carriage to push.

He is interested in the activity rather than in the result or what is made. He needs

— adults who encourage joyous fun, a good time during the process of work and play.

— adults who do not hamper him by stressing that he " make the picture exactly like this " or " be sure that the airplane wings are very smooth."

— adults who understand why he often is not interested in the picture or the clay object he has made.

He is able to concentrate in quiet activity for twenty to

thirty minutes. Therefore he needs

> — quiet times to balance active periods, when he may use tools for carpentry, the housekeeping center for home chores, puzzles to solve, and books to "read."

His mind

He is curious and asks many questions about things. Therefore he needs

> — to be answered correctly or helped to find answers to the extent of his ability for grasping information.

He can use complete sentences and give full information. Thus he needs

> — opportunities to talk with someone who is interested and who will listen attentively.

He is ready for facts, not fiction. He often asks, "Is it true?" He wants to know how things work. He needs

> — information about the fascinating world around him, not fairy tales.
>
> — books, pictures, and excursions to discover how everyday things work.

He thinks of a word in terms of what it does, such as "a spoon is to eat" and "a wagon is to ride." Therefore he needs

> — books, pictures, objects, and conversations that enrich his vocabulary and his thinking about meanings of words.

He can remember well. He needs

> — opportunities to recall an experience, to tell about it, to use new words, to use songs he has learned.

Usually he can print his first name, count by ones, distinguish traffic signals by their colors, name colors and pieces of money, and identify some cars and airplanes. He needs

> — opportunities to use such knowledge — to put his name on his papers, to tell the grownup when the traffic light permits them to cross, to talk about colors and money, to identify the machines in his world.

He is ready to learn the beginning of safety habits. Therefore he needs

> — simple rules for the kindergarten room and play space and streets.

He has very little sense of time except within a day's span. Past and future do not mean much. To him the important things are: Me, Here, and Now. Therefore he needs

> — activities in which he can imitate the daily life of the adults around him as they affect him — being the milkman, a storeman, Daddy at work, Mother in the kitchen, his church school teacher or the minister coming to call.

His attention span is increasing, so that he may pursue the same project for twenty to thirty minutes when keenly interested. Hence he needs

> — a variety of work materials and free time to try them, with adult guidance available if needed. Housekeeping and carpentry projects are absorbing interests.

He plans his work, can decide what he will do and do it, even carrying the plan over to the next day. So he needs

> — freedom to work on things at his own speed and time to finish them.
> — experiences in planning with a group and in carrying out the plan with the group.

He is critical of his own work and also that of his play-mates. He needs
> — to be shown the good points of work done.

His relationships with others

Mother is still the center of his life. Hence he needs
> — an understanding father and teachers who accept this fact without speaking of it and who do not make the child feel guilty about his preference.

Home is still his world. Therefore he needs
> — adults who help him in the transition from home to church and to school.
> — parents who visit and help on parents' committees of church and school.

He can begin to enjoy his younger sister and brother more than before. So he needs
> — actual experiences in helping them and in helping the younger children in the nursery department and the neighborhood.

He has a beginning interest in the community in which he lives. He should have
> — trips to the store, firehouse, library, bakery. Association with adults who contribute to his well-being in these and other places.

He can work in a group of two to four children as well as with one child. He needs
> — to be encouraged to work with others in increasing number.

He is friendly but can adjust to only a limited number of children or adults at one time. It is best that
> — kindergarten groups be kept as small as possible (twenty children at the most) with one teacher for every six or seven children.

He is interested in group activity. He needs

— materials that stimulate play in small groups, such as playing house, building a structure with blocks.

— freedom to carry out group ideas, with adults who are ready to help or answer questions but who are, for the most part, not in evidence.

He wants to conform — to do things "right," to act as others act. He often asks for approval: "Am I doing it right?" "Is this the way?" Therefore he needs

— approval of other children.

— adults who do not compare his progress with that of other children but with his own increasing ability.

He wants adult support and frequently asks for it. It is important that he have

— parents and teachers whom he can trust and on whose understanding he can depend.

He is not embarrassed by the affection of adults or children; he craves it. He needs

— warm, loving adults who are ready to praise and give him a pat or a hug.

— adults who do not make fun of children showing affection for one another.

He makes no differentiation between sexes but plays equally well with both boys and girls. He needs

— adults who permit this without separating boys from girls for work and playtimes.

— adults who do not tease or joke about play with the opposite sex. Boys need to play in the housekeeping center with dolls and kitchen equipment. Girls need to play with blocks and trucks.

He is bossy but can be co-operative and wait for his turn. So he needs

— opportunity to "boss" a small group in their

play and to " be bossed " by another child.

— to take turns in sharing work materials and toys and in playing games that provide for " wait until it is your turn."

He still quarrels and fights on occasion. Therefore he needs

— guidance about better ways of getting along with others, in having such ways pointed out to him when they occur.

— adults who will let him settle his own disputes.

He has a good sense of fair play. He needs

— adults who act fairly.

— encouragement in fair play.

He is becoming more independent and reliable. So he should be expected to

— care for his own belongings.

— share in caring for the work and play materials in the kindergarten.

He wants to help adults, but he resists things that are difficult and beyond him, rather than being challenged by them as he will be when older. He should have

— tasks within his ability so that he can feel he has done them well.

He really wants to do what the rest of the group does. He truly needs

— praise when he does act with the group.

— encouragement when he finds it more difficult.

He is not aware of racial, social, economic, or religious differences in children or adults. Therefore he needs

— to know various kinds of people in everyday life and to appreciate them as friends and helpers.

— parents and teachers who do not point out differences but who accept them as a normal part of life.

His feelings

Certain clearly defined emotions are developing; his responses are not as haphazard and momentary as before.

Pride. He needs

— something to be proud of, such as new shoes, a birthday, a new baby, approval of his accomplishments.

Shame. He needs

— the sense of disapproval by a person or a group when he speaks and acts unacceptably.

— adults who help him to understand why he acted so and to know that others have done the same.

— adults who help him to feel sorry for this act.

— adults who show they love him in spite of what he has done and expect him to do better next time.

Sympathy. Therefore he needs

— opportunities to give sympathy and love. He can understand those needs of others which are within his experience — hunger, sickness, and loneliness.

Happiness. He needs

— to express joy with others; to see them happy and share in fun together.

Seriousness. So he needs

— quieting, " man to man " talks with understanding adults on occasion.

Irritability. He needs

— adults who understand that he is irritable mainly when he is tired or not well.

— a rest period in any kindergarten session that is longer than one hour.

— quiet alternating with active periods both in kindergarten and at home.

Restlessness. He needs

— adults who understand that this indicates bore-
dom and lack of interest.

— freedom to change his choice of work or play.

Anxiety. He needs

— adults who realize that anxiety centers usually
about the availability of those he loves and on
whom he depends.

— reassurance, such as Mother's staying in a new
kindergarten or explaining where she will be when
she leaves.

How wonderful is the growth of a child! If we watch
him and listen to him carefully, he shows us his needs
without speaking directly about them. We can use this
chart of needs as a check on what we are doing with
and for children of this age. Do we parents and teachers provide the kinds of work materials, toys, room con-
ditions, atmosphere, experiences, and relationships that
are indicated? Are we doing and saying the particular
things that clear the way for and encourage wholesome
growth?

CHILDREN WHO ARE SPECIAL

Besides being aware of individuals having the typical
characteristics of growing four- and five-year-olds, we
must be alert to children that need us in a particular
way. There are some who have defective vision, speech,
or hearing; some who are left-handed; others who are
emotionally upset; some who are mentally slow or mentally superior. We may have to discuss with parents
whether or not a child needs professional help and discover ways we ourselves can best deal with him. We
can seek advice by reading books on " the exceptional
child," a term applied to those who need special care
for a variety of reasons.

It is especially important for a slow learner to be loved and accepted as he is and made to feel that he can do important things. We must foster his desire to try, to do, and help him to succeed. For the fast learner we must be sure to provide work materials that are sufficiently stimulating so he can experiment, solve problems with the materials, and learn relationships. We can encourage him to help other children in their work. He must be appreciated and encouraged but not kept in the limelight by always being the leader or planner. Children with special needs must be nurtured in particular ways.

BEFORE AND AFTER KINDERGARTEN AGE

In summary, let us look briefly at the growing child as he moves from three to six years of age — *before* and *after* he is kindergarten age. Most children of three have arrived at a stable period when they are eager to please and ready to do what is desired of them. They watch facial expressions to interpret what is wanted, and they are sensitive to praise when they have been acceptable to the adults around them. From this docile stage they gradually become bouncing four-year-olds who act and speak as they choose, seeming to fall head over heels in unusual behavior of body and mind. When they are about four, they are apt to ramble from one subject to another in conversation, and they do not care whether or not they finish an activity. But this too changes, and gradually they are again in a more stable period of growth. When they are about five, they are well-organized, self-contained, and at ease with themselves and the world. They can state a fact in conversation and stop there, not ramble. When they draw or paint, they determine what they will do, then do it. They are much concerned about completing what they begin.

It seems as if they have truly arrived, when again we see changes gradually taking place at about five and a half years or thereafter. A new phase begins when the child moves into the realm of elementary school. Here children seem once more at war with themselves and the world. They all want to be first; they all want to win; they all want the kind of fairness expressed in " an eye for an eye and a tooth for a tooth." Life is one constant conundrum, for it offers many new responsibilities, choices, and relationships. This is difficult, but it is another stage of change and growth.

To look at children in this progressive way helps both teachers and parents to understand that children have problems too. No later period of growth is marked by such rapid and dramatic changes as the first five years. Knowing this, we can live with our children more patiently, more lovingly, and more helpfully.

Chapter 2

HOW CHILDREN GROW
AND LEARN

It has been said that teaching takes place only when someone learns. If we would discover how to teach, we must first know how children learn. The previous chapter has indicated many of the growth patterns and needs of four- and five-year-olds. In the following snapshots from the life of Bobby we see how one child gradually learned about love and came to understand God's love.

Bobby was three years old when he said to his mother as he hugged her, " I love you three! " His mother tingled with excitement, for she knew that this was the utmost. Not one, nor two, but *three* — supreme quantity in Bobby's mind! She replied with another hug, " And I love you three! "

Now Bobby lived on a hillside where he could look out of the living room window and see many house tops. A few weeks later he ran to his mother saying, " I love you as many as all the houses."

Several months passed and summer vacation in the mountains brought new nighttime experiences with Mother and Father. Apparently his concept of quantity was growing, and again he linked it to his expression of love. The clear, bright stars presented an overwhelming vista, and one night after the family had been out in the dark to enjoy it, Bobby said, "Daddy, I love you as many as all the stars in the sky."

When Bobby was four, he heard his kindergarten teacher at church school say, "Let us love one another, for love is of God." Bobby was ready for those words and the experiences for showing love provided in the kindergarten room. But one Sunday he hit Alfred. The teacher stooped down, put her arm around him, and looked him straight in the eyes as she said: "That hurt Alfred, and I cannot let you hurt anyone. I love you, Bobby, but I do not like to see you hurt someone." Another aspect of love — one also experienced at home — was being reinforced in Bobby's mind: his teacher loved him even when he did something wrong!

Through these and many more experiences with parents, teachers, and friends, Bobby was learning what love means. He was learning by feeling, by watching, by imitating, by hearing, by speaking. His first experiences of love had to do with giving and receiving. As he grew older, he began to understand that the love he had known was a reflection of God's love. Now that he has become a man, he gives evidence of his concept of love by the way he is reflecting God's love with his own family and his fellow men. All of these experiences of learning comprise a concept of love understood and expressed on ever higher levels.

It would have been harder for Bobby to achieve a mature understanding of love if he had learned from his parents when he was young that their love was a reward for good behavior rather than a gift freely given. Somewhere in growing up he might have found the right idea, but the learning process would have been blocked for a time while he unlearned that early impression. Or if he had learned that love was only physical response without an accompaniment of comradeship and respect, he would again have been delayed while trying to learn the fullness of divine love. Thus it is possible for thoughtless adults to teach children things they have to unlearn later in life. Unlearning is a good deal harder than learning and sometimes causes such struggle within a person that he is unable to make the necessary adjustments for many years, if at all. It behooves parents and teachers to live their faith carefully if they would be sure that they are helping children in positive learning.

How Children Learn

For young children the process of learning occurs in many ways:

First, through the *senses*. From the moment of birth onward children learn by feeling, tasting, smelling, seeing, and hearing. A baby understands no words about love, but he begins to comprehend it through his feelings, his response to tone and touch. A small boy understands about chocolate through tasting and smelling before he knows the people and processes necessary to secure it. A little girl learns about the ocean by seeing and hearing and touching the waves. She cannot really understand its vastness nor where it goes no matter how hard we try to explain it. The whole body reaches out through its senses to absorb the world around it — to learn, to grow.

Secondly, by *imitating*. Along with seeing and hearing comes the urge to imitate. Even a four-year-old is often said to be " a chip off the old block." In his few short years he has learned to toss his head and walk just like his father. In the housekeeping center of the kindergarten the five-year-old girl cares for the doll family in ways very similar to those of her mother and neighbors. This means that parents and teachers must realize that what they are and do truly speaks louder than any words they say. Telling a child to be kind has no meaning whatsoever in the words alone. The child is busy doing exactly what the adults around him do and can only learn kindness through many unplanned observations and planned experiences that interpret kindness to him.

Thirdly, by *asking questions*. Probably every adult who lives with young children eventually comes to the time when he wearies of answering questions. Nevertheless, he patiently keeps on answering. He knows that children are curious about everything around them, and this curiosity helps them to learn. " What's this for, Daddy? How does it work? " " Let me smell too. Why does a flower smell that way? " Curiosity is natural to children. God gave them this wonderful characteristic which makes them reach out to learn. If they are answered politely and helpfully and encouraged later to find their own answers, children will retain this curiosity all their lives, and it will be a major asset in their work and well-being. Keep curiosity alive!

Fourthly, by *doing*. Curiosity is not limited to the asking of questions but includes experimenting as well. For instance, a child playing with blocks says to himself: " I wonder if this big block will stand on top of this little one. I'll try it and see." So he tries, and the tower of blocks falls over. He puts many blocks together in many ways and gradually learns the way to build a solid, sturdy tower. He tries and fails; he tries and succeeds. He would not learn to build a tower of blocks so well if an adult nearby always told him just how to do it. No, the child himself has to do the work and the thinking —

trying, discovering, experimenting, testing. Children learn through experiences.

Fifthly, through *hearing words* — associating the known to the unknown. Understanding spoken words is harder for a child than understanding the actions of the person who speaks. But there is a place for learning through information given in words. The teacher must be aware of the background experiences and the vocabulary of her young learners. Then as she presents information to them, she interprets it. For example, in a vacation church school unit, a teacher wanted to help her children understand that a church is not just a building but people — people doing certain things together. She began with the familiar part of the building, but also included new areas, such as the organ, pulpit, choir robing room, kitchen, and the people that use them. Pictures, excursions, and invited guests gave them information about the work of many people in the life of the church. Bible stories and passages showed why people build churches and what they do and learn in them.

Sixthly, by *using many ways* at the same time. One has only to watch a child for an hour to discover that the ways he learns are not set off in compartments but are all available to him at once — they overlap and intertwine. As we watch him, we marvel anew at the intricacies of human growth.

THE LAWS OF LEARNING

In and through the ways children learn, there are a few simple rules constantly operating. They are a guide to teachers and parents who plan good experiences of learning for children and are noticeable in common, everyday incidents of learning at any age. They are worded in many ways, but one commonly accepted is: the law of readiness, the law of effect, the law of practice or use.

For example, a professor learned to do cement work because his basement needed repairing. The cost of having the work done was exorbitant in proportion to his salary, so he decided to do it himself. This meant he was *ready* to learn something new. So he bought a book and studied how to do cement work. He talked with the man who sold him the materials. He experimented, did a small part, then the whole job. The *effect* was good, because his wife complimented him; he was satisfied with his accomplishment and with the saving of money. A few months later his brother needed help, so the professor used his new skill again. He was more adept at it this time and found the work easier as he taught it to his brother. This *practice or use* of the skill again impressed the learning more deeply on his mind and hands.

Time and again, in retrospect, when we analyze how we learned something, we find that first of all we wanted to learn it. We were physically able and mentally ready to learn; then the effect was good; we liked it and wanted to repeat it, so we practiced eagerly or used the new learning. These three steps produced an experience of learning.

Let us see how these laws of learning operated in the case of Bruce, who was brought to vacation church school by his grandmother. The teacher welcomed him and showed him many interesting things he might do in the kindergarten room, such as building blocks, using clay, painting at the easel, looking at picture books, working with trucks and cars. But Bruce chose to sit and watch. As the teacher welcomed other children, she

was aware of what each one chose to do. When it came
time to put away work materials and sit on the rug for
story time, she noticed that Bruce still sat on a chair to
watch. For an hour he seemed to be a spectator, but
then he joined the others for toileting, lunch, and rest.
When they went outdoors to play, he sat on the church
steps and watched. This pattern continued daily. One
of the teachers tried to include him by sitting near him
with the children who wanted to read books. If she put
her arm on the back of his chair, he would pull away.
Gently she would invite him to " come hear a story " or
" join the children for rhythms." Bruce would reply,
" Not me! " And thus eight days passed. The teachers
knew that Bruce was doing as well as he could and that
when he was ready he would do more. Sure enough, that
day came! Bruce joined the children in play and work
instead of watching them.

Before this time the teacher could see that Bruce was
not ready to be a part of the group in actually trying activities. He needed to watch. She was patient and
friendly, and finally *when he was ready*, he learned to
do what the other children did. The *effect of happiness*
at forgetting himself one day in the joy of story time
made his experience desirable and one to repeat. So he
repeated it day after day — first, only for story time, but
gradually he learned also to enjoy taking part in outdoor play, rhythms, and creative activities. Repetition,
which is practice or use, helped him learn it is good to
work and play with children. If the teachers had tried
to force Bruce to do just what other children were doing, he would have rebelled, been unhappy, and refused to attend vacation school. Such learning would
have been a negative experience. But by observing the
laws of learning, the teachers were able to work gradu-

ally and help Bruce through a positive learning experience.

THE LAW OF READINESS

There are times when adults want to prepare children for certain kinds of learning. For instance, there are occasional seasons when teachers hope that the children will assume responsibility for making the kindergarten room beautiful. One December morning four-year-olds arrived in a kindergarten department to find an untrimmed Christmas tree. Brightly colored papers and paste were on a nearby table. Instantly some of them chose to make decorations and put them on the tree. This experience followed all three laws of learning. The teacher had set the stage for the readiness that initiated the whole incident, and it was repeated the next session for further use of the new learning.

Another example of preparing children to learn is this. At home or church it is important for children to learn to put away toys and work materials. The adult explains in advance that when a certain time comes, it will be cleanup time, and everyone will help to put materials away in order to be ready to do something else. She gives them a warning a few minutes ahead; then she says, " Now is the time . . ." and they begin to work together. The adult does not command and direct but encourages and takes part. She makes it a gay and happy time of accomplishment. The children do it every day and become skillful at it. Because the adult observes the laws of learning, she helps the children move through a positive learning experience.

We have discussed two points relative to readiness:

> The natural readiness of a child, as in the case of Bruce.

Setting the stage or preparing a situation to help children become ready for a particular learning experience.

Both of these are important and both are understandable only when we study how a child grows and what he needs at each stage of growing (Ch. I). Teachers and parents of four- and five-year-olds must know each individual child in order to be aware of what he is ready to learn at a given time. We need to be sensitive to him — to see and feel what he needs so that we can say and do what is helpful. Sometimes we will plan experiences for him so that he finds himself in a certain situation with particular joys or problems.

In the kindergarten department of the church, we depend largely on denominational staff writers to plan experiences for our children. They have studied children and their needs in such a way that they can determine long-range goals and develop a curriculum that is suitable to a growing person of this age. We use the printed curriculum and adapt it to meet the needs of our particular children. We do not force every child to do everything that is printed in the materials. For as we have seen, learning cannot be forced. The learner must be ready.

THE LAW OF EFFECT

This law is the measure of a learning experience in terms of satisfaction or dissatisfaction. Although much learning, good or bad, goes on without adult knowledge or supervision, often the difference is dependent upon the parent or teacher who is close at hand. The attitude and manner of the adult are frequently responsible for creating an effect that is positive or negative. Consider the example of learning to pick up toys and work materials as given under " The Law of Readiness." The adult can make this a drab, unhappy experience by what she does and says. If she scolds and prods, the child does not feel good about the experience. But if she herself puts "this red car in this garage" and "the blue car in the parking lot" and "the tiny blocks all huddled together," her imaginative talk and her comradeship in the act of doing is encouraging to the child and makes the whole experience fun.

All of us learn best when we are in a place where we know we are wanted. We grow best where we are loved, where others are interested in the things we say and do. If this be true of older people, how much more it is true for young children who are as sensitive as barometers to the atmosphere around them.

Watch a child come to a strange place such as the kindergarten room on his first Sunday. How does he feel? Is he wanted here? Suppose he finds a smile; an invitation to look around the room to discover just what he may want to do; someone to look at a picture book and enjoy it with him; friendly children who are laughing together, listening to music, building blocks, talking, watching quietly. If the child feels free to do the things that appeal to him, he feels good about the whole situation. Such satisfactions indicate that he will grow and learn happily.

On the other hand, let a child come to this strange room and be asked to " sit still until time to begin." He is puzzled. This is the most difficult thing that could be required of him — to sit still! Then he asks a question and the reply is, " Just a minute, dearie, I have to get out our crayons and paper." He sees one adult look at another with a frown as she separates two squealing children clutching one truck. He is not sure he wants to be in this place. The law of effect operates here also, and if he is forced to come to this room, what kind of growing will take place? Monty went to such a room and after three weeks he stood up tall and said to his mother, " I'd like to take all the Sundays and hide them behind the world." He refused to go to church school.

Children are like plants. They respond to their environment with healthy, sturdy growth or with frail, stunted growth. It is adults who provide the environment and make the climate for effective learning in the kindergarten. A good climate exists when the adult conscientiously tries to see the child's viewpoint: to feel what he may be feeling deep down inside; to answer his questions honestly but briefly; to be interested with him in little joys. Because children imitate freely, this warm friendliness of the teacher begins to exist between child and child as well as between adult and child, and *effective* learning goes on at an amazing pace.

The Law of Practice or Use

After taking into account the laws of readiness and effect as parts of the learning process, a teacher must then help children use what they have learned. Perhaps she has sung a song to the children several times, and they have gradually joined her until they know it too. She will help them remember it by using it often. That is, the song could well be used more than once during a morning session, certainly every day in vacation school, and every Sunday for several weeks in Sunday church school — at points where it is relevant or fits the situation.

The teacher helped the four-year-olds who decorated their Christmas tree to use their new skills and attitudes in decorating their room on later occasions, such as Valentine Day and Easter.

Information is really absorbed and new ideas or concepts formed only as they are repeated again and again in different ways. So it was with the teacher (described on page 31) who helped her group learn much that was new to them about their church. Later she encouraged the children to use their information in a variety of ways. Long after the first experiences were past, she guided them in expressing their ideas about the church through their play and work activities. Families in the housekeeping center played " going to church." Drawings and paintings told about the colors in the windows. Their block-building developed into more complicated structures as one day the teacher said, " This church is empty." " It needs some people," said Hugh as he went to the shelf for the stand-up figures. The teacher said: " There is only one room in this church. Where do the mothers and fathers meet? " The children had a delightful time enlarging their block church with partitions for rooms and people of different sizes in those rooms. Day after day they used their new information about their church in many ways.

Time was when teachers thought they had to provide a box of crayons for each child in the kindergarten. But with fewer boxes they have found that two children are often put in a position to take turns with the colored crayon they both wish to use. Then they learn to take turns with one dump truck, one doll carriage, one broom and dustpan. Teachers make it possible at many times for children to practice or use the new learning of taking turns so that they will really learn it well.

In Summary

A child of kindergarten age is constantly learning and growing. He explores his world and seeks to understand it with his whole being. God has provided people — parents, teachers, relatives, friends — to guide and help him as best they are able. We try to understand his needs. We study to improve our ways. We learn and grow even as he learns and grows. We try to be clear channels through which God may speak to the young child; simultaneously we find God speaking to us through that child. God works within us both. A doctor whose experience has been in helping patients mentally as well as physically has put it this way: "What is a child? You cannot describe him without thinking of the whole life of the man, with all its unknowns, for which he is preparing. . . . There is always some mystery remaining, arising from the very fact that the person is alive. We can never know what new upsurge of life may transfigure it tomorrow. . . . We can help. . . . But the essential aid, that which touches the person, its awakening and growth, can come only from God." [1]

[1] From *The Meaning of Persons,* by Paul Tournier. Used by permission of Harper & Brothers, publishers.

Chapter 3

WAYS OF CHRISTIAN NURTURE

Philip was in the hospital seven times before he was four years of age! When he was enrolled in the church kindergarten, his mother explained to the teachers what he had been through, and they agreed that Mother would attend with Philip as long as he needed her. She came for eight Sundays, and on the ninth she sat in the hall near the door. Philip brought a stuffed animal with him that day and continued to do so for three months. He clung to it continually but finally put it down while he worked, and one Sunday he appeared without it. What had happened? From a fearful, insecure child, he unfolded ever so slowly into a happy, steady child. His parents and teachers had worked carefully and patiently in many ways. How had they taught him? How had they helped him grow in confidence? Briefly, they were aware of Philip's personal needs and cognizant of his special kind of four-year-oldness; they understood how a child learns; they had a purpose in mind as they worked. Glance back at the preceding chapters; in them are the essentials to keep in mind as we prepare to teach.

There are many ways of teaching children, but the ways that make for the best growth are those wherein the parent or teacher acts as a guide and moves with children through shared experiences. She may be on hand for casual happenings between children, or she may plan certain experiences for them. She seeks to become sensitive in knowing just how much she is needed, when she should speak, and when she should refrain from speaking in order to permit the maximum learning to take place. She is aware of the kind of noise that means all is well and the kind that indicates unhappiness. She seeks to become more skillful at

listening — to hear all that a child wants to say.

watching — to see what he tells about himself by his actions and to help when guidance is needed.

speaking — to express approval and friendship without sentimentality; to give necessary directions slowly and softly, but firmly.

singing — to express immediate thought and feeling.

sharing — to enjoy the little things that are so new and exciting to a child.

talking — to suggest ways of working and playing, to tell a story, to read a book, to read the Bible, to pray, to interpret experience by a casual comment or question.

All of this is teaching, no matter what particular method or technique is being used. The discussion of ways of guiding children in Christian nurture in this and the two succeeding chapters will give further insight into the part the teacher and parent must take.

CONVERSATION

Conversation is a vital part of life in the kindergarten. It weaves in and through all aspects of a teaching session and is valuable in many ways, both in church school and home.

By the time children are four and five, they have acquired fairly large vocabularies and are eager to be sociable through talking with one another and with adults. They talk about things they have experienced, what they have heard or seen, smelled, touched, or tasted. Many times they ask questions simply to engage an adult in friendly conversation. They enjoy the sounds of words and phrases and experiment in creating them — a process at which an adult should not show amusement, except to join in the fun of words that rhyme and sing. They imitate readily and will use new words (often correctly) before they really understand their meanings. This perplexes parents and teachers who, not knowing that meanings are missing, give credit for knowledge the children do not have. Correspondingly, children who do not speak often know and understand more than we realize. They may live with adults who believe that " children should be seen and not heard " and are therefore not permitted to talk much. Or they may live in the shadow of an older and wiser brother or sister, so they are ignored or " squelched."

Individual conversation between child and teacher is especially important. When the child arrives at the kindergarten room, he shares personal happenings with his teacher-friend. If she will listen more than she speaks, she will find that a few questions can open the way to a child's mind and heart. This give-and-take between grownup and child builds friendship and understanding.

Group conversation is encouraged at story time — when the children discuss a picture, when they share things they have made, when they recall an excursion they took together, when they eat midmorning lunch, when they talk of what they did yesterday in order to share it with someone who was absent. Often all the children wish to talk at once. But with adult patience and fairness the children can learn to listen to one another and to take turns at talking. The following group conversation occurred in a Sunday church school when a teacher tried to explain a Bible verse.

The four-year-olds had had an informal playtime, then had come together in a group and sat down on the rug around the teacher. She began to sing,

> " Every morning seems to say,
> ' There's something happy on the way,
> And Gods sends love to you! ' "

The children joined her and they sang the song twice. She opened her Bible and read, " ' God cares about you.' "

Then she said: " God sends love to you because he cares about you. One way that God sends his love is by planning for people to live together in families. He plans for fathers and mothers to take care of children."

" My mommy and daddy take care of me," said Florence.

" So do my mommy and daddy." " And so do mine! " " And so do mine! "

The teacher continued, " God planned for grandparents to help care for children too."

" My grandmother lives at my house," said Donald.

" I don't have a grandmother," offered Timmy.

" I have a baby at my house," volunteered Mary.

The teacher went on: " Babies need special care. Boys and girls who are four and five can help Mother take care of baby. That would be one way God would send love to the baby."

Tommy, an only child of middle-aged parents, said: "We don't have a baby. But my mommy says that someday I might have a baby. All of us [and he made a wide gesture with his arm] will have babies. We'll all be mommies and daddies someday."

"That's right, Tommy," replied the teacher. "That is the way God plans for families. Children grow big and tall, and later they become mommies and daddies. Do you remember the words in the Bible that tell us why God makes good plans for each one of you? Let me read them to you: 'God cares about you.' Let's say that together: 'God cares about you.'" The teacher thanked God in prayer for his love and care. Then the children all stood with her to sing the song again.

In many group conversations the teacher asks questions to stimulate thinking. She may ask questions to see if the children understand a story just told. She must word her questions carefully so that they cannot always be answered by yes or no. She will learn to arrange her questions in logical sequence in order to guide the children in thinking through an issue or in planning a piece of work. She will help the talker to listen more. She will encourage the less talkative to express himself and will recognize his contributions to the group. She will pronounce words clearly and use new words as needed, words that she explains in some way or that grow out of a shared experience. The teacher will provide good books and poetry, rhymes, jingles, and stories. She will be alert to record rhythmical sounds and interesting or poetic ideas that come from the children at unexpected moments of work and play. Children will respond eagerly to the stimulus she provides in these ways. They will imitate and practice, soon learning more and more about how to talk with one another and with adults.

This may be a necessary beginning to their ability when grown to witness to their faith. How can a person possibly obey Jesus' last specific command unless he has learned to communicate to others his purposes and hopes, his deepest thoughts, and most dearly held beliefs?

PLAY

Children are always ready for play, and they learn most naturally through it — exploring, thinking, doing. And although we adults may call what they are doing " play," to the child it is his work — the stuff of which life is made. We define the word " play " in terms of leisure and relaxation. A child's play is more like an adult's hard work, for in it he plans, tries, fails, tries again, succeeds. So we must not minimize the use of play in our teaching plans. Play is our ally in helping children learn many things.

Through play a child can express his hidden desires. He discovers early in life that it must be wonderful to be an adult, to " be big," to be " grown up." So in his play he becomes that adult! He spanks the doll children; he goes off to work with his lunch pail; he bakes a cake; he sweeps the floor. As a child watches others use certain tools he wishes to master them also. So he tries to use scissors, hammer, or paintbrush. As he watches grownups go to meetings, so too he will go. Two little girls in dress-up clothes left the housekeeping center and went to the far side of their kindergarten room. As they walked back, the teacher heard one say to the other, " I didn't like that PTA meeting, did you? "

Through play a child tries to solve his problems. He

may feel unhappy and insecure and take his feelings out on someone or something, as the child did who shook the doll and said, " Now you eat your food." Perhaps he knocks down blocks, pounds the clay, hits and kicks. He tries to join in the play of others or sulks apart from them. If the former, he may offer ideas, or he may just grab what he wants in an effort to be accepted.

Through play a child learns how to live harmoniously with others. He finds out what is his and what is not his. He discovers that other people have feelings and ideas too and that he can engage in worth-while activities with them. He learns about himself and his relationship to people; he develops attitudes and habits in dealing with people.

Play may be enjoyed all alone, with other children, with adults. Play uses the things at hand: sticks, pebbles, cars, sand, dolls. It uses the minds of those who play — creatively, happily, sociably, antagonistically. Play uses the bodies in swift movement, gentle rhythms, immobility. It uses the spirits of those who play as they experience shared delight, united purpose, sensitive wondering. Play is the eager work of children.

After realizing the value of play for children's growth, parents and teachers have a definite responsibility: they must provide the space, the right materials, the time, and often guidance. Chapter 6 deals with space and materials. Adults must protect the children so that they will have uninterrupted time to use the space and materials freely within limits. They must then be on the side lines to help clarify ideas, develop deeper meanings, add new information, sort out reasons for disputes, protect the rights of each child, join in their imaginative " let's pretend." The patience and understanding, affection and interest the adult reflects as she shares these experiences are directly related to her own acceptance of " love one another."

Informal Play

Informal play is that part of a session in which a child feels free to choose any available activity that he desires. It usually occurs at the beginning of a session and is referred to as " working in interest centers." It is valuable for a child to have such a time to look around at the toys and equipment in the kindergarten room; to try out different materials; to talk with children his own age; to choose for himself what he will do next. A free period at the opening of the session permits each child to fit into the larger group at his own speed. Some will need the entire time for several days to look around before they will feel at ease in doing things with others. The same kind of situation exists when a child is a guest or has a guest in the home.

Teachers can learn much about children in this free play period if they watch them and do not suggest what they are to do and how they are to do it. *Too much teacher* (or too much parent) spoils the free and happy play of children and delays the growth that can take place when they settle their problems satisfactorily with one another. Note carefully what the children do: some will start immediately to build with blocks or play house; some will walk around the room trying many things; some will just sit and watch.

Not enough teacher is just as hard on a group of children in a free time of work and play as too much teacher. In this period of observing your children, you will get acquainted with each one if you concentrate on them as individuals and jot down notes to help you remember. Each child needs, particularly those in the following list, you to step in and help him in a special way.

The child who grabs what he wants when he wants it. Be on the spot when that child grabs. " What do we do when we want a certain block? " you ask the children who are building. " Wait our turn," and " Ask the one who has it if we can have it now," come the replies. " But grabbing is not a good way," you say without a scolding tone, touch, or look, looking directly at the " grabber " so that he knows you mean him. Then be ready to commend him when you later see that he waited his turn or asked permission.

The child who flits around without finishing anything. By sharing his activity, help this child stay with one thing until it is finished. You may look at a picture book, build a house, or fit together a puzzle. Avoid undue pressure but help him find satisfaction in completing things.

The child who annoys others and disrupts what they are doing. When this child pinches, kicks, or pushes over a tower of blocks, talk with him and the others involved: " Kicks and pinches hurt. I cannot let any child in this room hurt another child or spoil what another child is doing." Again, you look the offender directly in the eyes — with kindness but with decision. If blocks have been pushed over, stoop down to the children and ask: " Who should be the one to push over the blocks? " " That's right — the one who makes the tower has the right to push it over. When someone else wants to do it, he must ask if he can or ask if you can do it together." If two children are excited and upset about a " fight," it will probably help to take them away from the others to a quiet place to calm down and talk it over.

The child who stands passively at the side. Let this child feel that you are his friend through an occasional

smile or word of encouragement. Much talking or coax-
ing will not help him; often the best help is to let him
watch. Take something to him, such as a book to read
together, a puzzle to share, or perhaps a child to work
with him. Gradually he can be led to another part of the
room where other work and play is taking place. Jon
went through the motions of participation for ten days
in weekday church school before becoming involved as
a real part of the group. He always seemed to be de-
tached, but finally a fun story before rest period brought
him down from his chair on the edge of the group to a
place on the rug right in front of the teacher. For the
first time he seemed completely at ease and at one with
the children.

*The child who wants to do something but cannot get
started.* Give this child an extra word of assurance: " You
can do it any way you like "; " It's such fun to do
this! " Patty was very particular about being neat and
clean; she seemed to fear the messiness of finger paint.
She needed help to " let go " as she stood at the table
where others were finger painting. The teacher said to
her: " Your paper is all wet and ready for the paint,
Patty. What color will you use first? " Then later: " Isn't
that color pretty? And doesn't the paint feel soft and
squishy? I like it in my hands, don't you? " Some boys
fear to play with dolls because of ridicule at home.
They need to be reminded that daddies care for babies
just as mothers care for them: " They dress them and
hold them gently and take them for a walk."

The child who never helps to put away materials.
Work next to this child during cleanup time and encourage him to work with you. Help him to enjoy it and to
appreciate the accomplishment of making the room

neat. Take pains to let his parents know that the children in the kindergarten pick up and put away their things.

The child who has ideas and gets busy right away. Ask him questions and talk about his work so that his ideas grow from day to day. Bobby was a natural builder; he made a flour mill one day, a bridge the next, a church (with two others helping him) on the third day. His teacher said: " I am a mother bringing my little girl to the kindergarten in your church. To which room will I take her? " " We don't have any rooms in this church," Bobby replied. " You might put rooms in your church," added the teacher, and she left the three busy with rebuilding in order to add rooms.

The child who directs others in a group of two or three. Encourage this child who bosses to accept the ideas of other children even as he directs those who are not used to the feeling of group play. Nancy was a splendid "mother" in the housekeeping corner. Every day she did the chores and bossed the others who played there. The teacher suggested that Kenneth be the father. Kenneth had ideas too; so Nancy had to learn to give and take. The teacher went to call at this " home." " Good afternoon, Mother Nancy," she said. " I have come to tell you that the lady in the house over there is very sick and needs you to help her." This started further thinking toward neighborliness.

Guiding informal play may be the hardest part of your teaching job in the kindergarten. But *work* at it. Watch your children and try to interpret aright the things they do. Watch the words that you say lest you get in a rut and use phrases that do not necessarily promote growth. For instance:

Do not always say this:
" What do you want to do today? "

> *Instead,* " Here is the clay waiting for someone to pound it."

" Why don't you play house? "

> *But,* "I think I hear that baby doll crying. Probably she wants her breakfast."

" What is this you have made? "

> *Rather,* "Tell me about it — it looks so interesting."

" That's nice."

> *But,* " The part with the window is *so* nice."

" I like that."

> *Instead,* " You have done a good job. I like it, don't you? "

Keep notes about particular children whom you want to know and help in a special way. Day by day, the story will unfold and you will find joy in seeing actual growth in individual children.

Free play offers a vital way of growing for four- and five-year-olds. Work hard at knowing when you are *too much* teacher or *not enough* teacher, and be just the *right* teacher in guiding such growth.

Dramatic Play

A child feels utter freedom in " playing " anything or anybody. He forgets himself and actually becomes an animal, a truck driver, a parent, a doctor, or a policeman. His imagination provides properties and costumes. Through his actions and spoken words, he reveals his ideas about a given role, his feelings and attitudes toward it. If he is playing father or mother, he shows what he understands about that role and what exists in his relationship to his own parents. A mother listening in to her children playing house may see herself mirrored and pause to rebuke herself for a careless action or to be grateful for an incident of thoughtful patience. If a child is playing the role of truck driver, he is learning a skill by practicing it; he is steering his big truck through the traffic of the kindergarten room. If he plays farmer, he practices running a tractor, hoeing a garden, or picking apples and squash. Besides revealing his understanding and practicing skills, he gains new information. For example, David had never ridden on a ferryboat, but in the kindergarten he learned much about ferries from his play with Paul whose grandfather often took him on ferryboat excursions. In a similar way, Byron learned something about fathers by watching others take the part. Because he and his divorced mother lived with grandparents, he would always take the role of grandfather in the housekeeping center. In every kindergarten session dramatic play takes place during informal playtime in the housekeeping and building centers. It may also take place after the children hear a story and wish to " play " it. Fours and fives are casual about taking parts and play a story best when all can be in it and act without lines or planned speaking parts. Each acts as he wishes to interpret the story. Through dramatic play also, the children can explain what they understand about a song, a picture, a Bible verse, a poem. Teachers may suggest such play and then help to correct misunderstandings that come to light.

On an especially hot summer day one teacher used dramatic play to quiet a group of restless children in vacation school. After lunch period, when they had cleaned their tables and put down their mats, she invited them to sit around her. " Summertime is the time when beautiful butterflies are seen flying lightly in our yards and gardens. Let's pretend that we are butterflies today. I know a song that tells about butterflies opening their wings, flying to the garden, smelling the roses and hollyhocks, then flying home. The very end of the song says, ' fold your wings gently and rest.' Listen and I will sing the song to you; then we will all play we are butterflies when I sing it again." Of course, at the end of the song each flew down to his own resting mat. She found that this simple play helped the children to forget their desire to be at work. They *became* butterflies, forgot themselves, and relaxed quickly for a much-needed rest.

The part of the parent or teacher in dramatic play with children is first of all to enjoy the make-believe world of childhood. If you did not enjoy it as a child, try to understand it now so that you can permit your children to find delight in it. If you have a spirit sensitive to make believe, you can enter into their play in such a way that they know you are going along with them and having fun too. Just a comment to " the doctor," not Ted, to the " store clerk," not Jane, helps a child know that you are " in it." He continues in his role with new joy and abandon. Make it known to the children that there is no right way in this experience. Everyone can make believe his own way; then it is sure to be a good way. This is encouraging to one who may be corrected many times in his daily life! In dramatic play he is on his own; he can act as he sees fit and is helped thereby to meet real life situations later. Sometimes make-believe clothes are helpful. A man's hat and shirt may help some boys to become " Father " more realistically. When the whole group plays the story of the shepherds going to see the baby Jesus, they may feel the story more completely if they put on a headpiece or scarf of Palestinian type.

What value do adults — we who are parents or neighbors, the minister or superintendent who drops in to visit the kindergarten on Sunday morning — place on children's play? Their " play " may not seem of much consequence or worth to us, but if we listen to their account of it, we can express genuine appreciation of their efforts.

GAMES

To many children in a kindergarten the idea of games in a large group is entirely new, for most of their play has been informal and individual. As they hold hands in a circle or move together in participation, games help them begin to sense what a group is like. They experience group pleasure or displeasure as the group helps them take part in acceptable ways.

Use the simplest games with a new group of children, and add more difficult ones later. As children become acquainted throughout the year, they can do a better job of playing a game than they did when they first tried it. Games should have only two or three directions, and the teacher must realize that not all the children will understand them until the game is played several times. The best games for this age provide participation for all or most of the children simultaneously. " Drop the handkerchief " is a poor game, for only two can take active part, and the others lose interest. In " Here We Go Round the Mulberry Bush " all may participate. " The Farmer in the Dell " permits all to play, with several having special parts. The words to these two singing games can be adapted to fit units of study in the curriculum. Competition is not stressed in preschool games, but rather the fun of all taking part, evidenced in the games that children themselves invent. Whether indoors or outdoors, active or quiet, imitative or more thought-provoking, games furnish basic learning for living.

APPRECIATION

Taking time to look at flowers and stones, to hear wind and birds, to smell phlox and clover, is important for children. When we watch them in their leisure, we see that they take time for little things. Adults must take time with them, realizing that what is ordinary to us is brand-new to them. They live in the expectancy of discovery — in a world full of interesting things just for them to explore. When a child brings a strange bug or worm, be interested in it. When he brings a common ordinary rock, be glad to see it. Help him to appreciate that only God can make a bug or a rock. Take time also to listen to lovely music, to enjoy a beautiful picture, to tell over and over again a favorite Bible story, to look at sunshine on stained-glass windows or blue sky through clear windows, to taste crisp crackers and cool water, and to make new friends. While some appreciation comes through the mind, most comes through the senses. This is especially true for children, and we can develop within them keen appreciation if we share their enthusiasms and plan for new experiences.

With older friends we usually hear appreciation expressed in words or see it in acts of kindness. But in children it comes as an exclamation — a sigh — a smile! Words are too new and too few for expressing emotions. Sometimes there is no way of even knowing how the child feels; but life is so rich for the growing person who is sensitive to things and people that we would covet many experiences with them for every child.

Let us consider some of the *things* we help children to appreciate in the kindergarten — objects, pictures, books, music — and then people to appreciate.

First, we want them to be curious about nature — all that God has made. A close touch with nature is common to many children but almost unknown to others. The teacher of city children often needs to bring nature into her room — moss from the woods, seed pods, autumn leaves, good earth, seeds and bulbs for planting, guinea pigs, chickens, cocoons. The teacher of rural children must interpret the ordinary and point up its special beauties and intricacies in terms of God's wondrous plans.

Then there are other areas of enjoyment, such as objects from another land. On a very hot day an unusual fan from a faraway land is admired and appreciated. One teacher showed her children a collection of dolls in varied dress, and they were eager to handle them tenderly. But unfortunately she added: "When you come up to see them, don't touch. I know its a temptation, but don't touch them." Another teacher took a straw ball from Thailand to her kindergarten room. How the children loved this "woven ball with holes in it"! Later she took a small, carved animal because the wood was so mellow and pleasing to the touch. She knew her children would enjoy it.

In our use of pictures we want some to be appreciated for their beauty and others for what they say. There is an old Chinese proverb that tells us, "One picture is worth a thousand words." If this be true, how carefully we must choose the pictures for a kindergarten room! The best are simple and colored. They have only a few figures and little detail so that the central idea is conveyed clearly. From four to six years of age a child grows considerably in his ability to see what is in a picture.

Teaching pictures that are purchased with the church curriculum and appropriate magazine pictures may be trimmed and mounted on uniform oak tag or colored construction paper that blends with the pictures. They are used more readily when filed by subjects, such as Family, Church, Nature, Christmas, and Easter. Pictures related to each session can be placed on a picture rail, hung on a screen or wall, arranged on a table for children to handle, supported by table easels, or fastened with paper clips to a taut wire stretched wherever convenient. Or a particular picture may be slipped into a picture frame without glass for the day's use. All must be placed on the eye level of the children.

Pictures are used in many ways: after a story, before a story, with Bible verses, with songs, to stimulate conversation, to suggest attitudes, for introducing a new subject, in suggesting ways of acting with one another, for pure enjoyment.

Many church school teachers are negligent in their use of picture books. The joy of reading good books is begun in preschool years when children learn to respect books and handle them with care. Books that interpret the purposes in the year's curriculum should be purchased. A list of such books is usually available from denominational curriculum editors. Begin with a few in the fall and add to the supply as the year progresses. Books may be kept in a rack similar to a magazine rack so that children can see the cover pictures for identification. They may be kept in a small bookcase, on a shelf, or broad window sill, depending upon the quantity used and the space available. Wherever kept, books should have a special place with chairs for the readers. In developing an appreciation for books, the child learns best from the adults around him — from their interest and pleasure in the use of books.

Music can be appreciated in so many ways! Some of these ways are discussed under " Music."

Let us also think of ways to appreciate *the worth of people*. All of us long to be recognized, to be loved, to be considered important, to receive sympathy in illness and mishap, to find others happy in our good fortune. Whether a regular member, a newcomer, or a visitor, each child should be welcomed personally in a warm and friendly way. The old-time manner of singing " Good Morning to You " and " Sunday School Is Over " was rather a formal substitute for personal attention. Lighting candles on a wooden birthday cake pointed up attention all right, but what kind? Today the birthday child is appreciated for how he has grown and what he can do, as the teacher thanks God for him in a birthday prayer. Grownups who work in the church — minister, organist, sexton, and secretary — become the children's friends. Their work is valued, and the children are enlisted to help them in carefully planned ways. There can be a new baby, an illness, a trip, new shoes; the sharing of big and little experiences builds a fellowship of church friends. All this — caring, esteeming, being grateful — is appreciation, and appreciation of people leads to loving them. Christians are especially sensitive to people; we accept and love one another because God accepts and loves us. " He first loved us," so in his love we learn to love. This is the goal toward which we lead our children as we help them to appreciate the wonder of things and of people.

Caring about people in sad and glad times leads to

expressing one's love by doing something for them. Letting another child play with his toys is a beginning of sharing for the young child. Then gradually, after he has known the pleasure of owning his very own books and toys, the child will come to the day when he is able to give away a personal possession for someone else's pleasure. This is a long, slow process to our adult eyes, but we must let it be as slow as is necessary for each individual child. Most children are not ready for sharing or giving at kindergarten age. But adults can help them learn to give by guiding them in making gifts, such as a drawing, a table mat, or a clay object. These things will have more meaning for them than gifts purchased with money, for any money a child has is given to him by adults. He cannot possibly understand what it means to earn money nor can he comprehend its value or power. Usually he uses it as he is told. Giving money to the church is a habit we wish to start early, but one which has little meaning, except as a child shares in something the whole family does. Hence, it is important for teachers in the church school to make it possible for children to give gifts of things they can make, things that they themselves enjoy, services needed by people they are interested in. Where money itself is concerned, it is important for parents and teachers to interpret to the child gifts given through the church.

Besides individual gifts there are group gifts. Twenty children in a vacation school went to call on an older friend who was shut in and took her songs and stories and Bible verses they knew, planning in advance what they would share. Another department planted bulbs in January and took the flowering plant to their minister. Many groups make get-well cards for children who are sick and simple toys for the nursery department.

Chapter 4

WAYS OF CHRISTIAN NURTURE (continued)

WORSHIP

The visitor in the kindergarten department was puzzled by what she had observed one winter morning. "Now we'll have our worship," the leader said when it was time to put away work and play materials and sit by the piano. There was considerable restlessness as some waited for others to arrive. The leader began by asking, "What songs would you like to sing today?" The children sang the usual requests; then the leader asked the girls to sing alone, next the boys. After this she said: "Both were good. I could hardly tell which was the loudest. Now let's say a little prayer. I think it would be so nice. Fold your hands, bow your heads, and close your eyes." The teacher prayed, and the children repeated the prayer after her. Next came a story, and then she read a Bible verse from her curriculum book.

Was it "worship" as the teacher had said? How had God been honored in that time? What feelings did the children have toward him? Can worship be commanded at a set time? Or is it something that best occurs in any and all parts of the kindergarten session? What should be the reason for praying? What is a "little" prayer? Should all praying be done with bowed heads and folded hands? How will children come to know and love the Bible if it is not used in their presence?

We adults go to a Sunday morning church service to worship God. Because of our past experiences and information, we know why we go and what we intend to do. The very word worship conveys to us praising, honoring, seeking, confessing, giving. But even though we know what we intend to do, do we actually worship? The honest answer is yes and no. Probably few people maintain a sense of worship the entire time they are in the service. One person feels great joy and overwhelming gratitude in the prelude, hymn, invocation, and Gloria Patri. Another feels deep regret and seeks forgiveness in the pastoral prayer and hymn of consecration. Another may have gone through all of this in rote fashion with her mind on her children and the dinner, but during the sermon it seemed as if the minister spoke directly to her, and she was moved deeply in regard to her responsibility as a member of the church of God.

If the meaning of worship varies for adults in a given hour, must it not be even less clearly defined for children? Yet it is our privilege to help children learn through worship how to respond to God, the Creator. It is not enough that in the church kindergarten children learn to play well together, to share work materials, and to think through problems. It is not enough that they hear a story, beautiful music, and passages from the Bible. We must somehow help them to begin to understand

> *that we are all God's people* and that God has planned the way for us to live together in love and forgiveness as families and as church families.

that this is God's wonderful world — a fact before
which we stand in awe and wonder.
that God loved us so much that he sent Jesus to tell
and show us the greatness of that love — a gift to
which we respond in love and gratitude.
*that we must learn to think about God often and
pray to him.*

Wonder, gratitude, love, forgiveness — here are the elements of worship (not merely the forms through which
they are expressed) that we must keep in mind as we
work with children.

Someone has said, "Religion is caught, not taught,"
and that is one way of saying that worship must perme-
ate all that a teacher is and does and says in the kindergarten room. One teacher, who was trying to help her
children worship, analyzed one of her sessions. As
nearly as she could tell, real worship occurred for Tonya
when she was smelling and arranging some orange day
lilies, and the teacher prayed: "O God, Tonya and I are
so glad to have these flowers in our church today. Thank
you, thank you, God!" For Freddy, worship seemed to
be during the time he looked at the pictures in *Small
Rain* with another teacher, leisurely turning the pages
and reading the Bible verses that were illustrated. For
Hortense, it was a picture — a magazine picture showing an orchard with a rainbow. For Tom and John, it
was the thoughtful, quieting talk with the teacher after
they had begun a fist fight. Part of these experiences
she had planned — not the fight, of course! (But she
was ready for it, for she had thought through what she
would do in such a case.) She had brought the lilies and
laid them on a newspaper for someone to choose to arrange. She had asked her assistant to select books re-

lated to the day's purpose. When she had found the ex-
quisite rainbow picture and recognized its possibilities
for her children in the church, she had mounted it for
her file.

In a similar fashion teachers and parents plan for worship experiences in these ways:

> They plan for beauty, order, and cleanliness in the
> room — not perfectionism in housekeeping, but a
> sense of " This room is what our children know as
> their church. It must be as lovely as we can make
> it."

> They neatly arrange pictures that further the day's
> purpose.

> They use experiences with nature — planting seeds,
> watering plants, arranging flowers, feeding gold-
> fish, turtles, or birds, taking outdoor walks, looking
> out the window at snow and rain, listening to the
> wind, looking through a magnifying glass at a blue
> feather or purple clover. A wonder table or beauty
> corner encourages children to seek and bring na-
> ture objects, all of which can be interpreted as the
> work of God, the Creator.

> They watch for joyous relationships between chil-
> dren to point out God's will that we love and help
> one another.

> They watch for unhappy times when a child may
> need to learn to say, " I'm sorry," and another to re-
> ply, " It's all right now."

> They arrange for song-story-picture-conversation-
> prayer-song in a way that children are led to feel
> and say, " Thank you, thank you, God! " " I love

you, God "; " I wonder how he made it [a pebble] ";
" I wonder how it [a turtle] works! "

They use the Bible in a way that reflects their love
of it, their belief in it, their dependence upon it.

They look for opportunities that lead to prayer in
the things children are doing.

They recognize that in worship, silence sometimes
means more than the spoken word.

G. K. Chesterton has said, " The world will never
starve for want of wonders but only for want of wonder." It is both true and sad that the exuberant curiosity
and wonder of childhood is somehow lost for many as
they become young people and adults. Teachers and
parents can help children keep this spontaneous joy by
encouraging it and by themselves being alert to new discoveries. Rachel Carson, author of *The Sea Around Us*
and *The Edge of the Sea*, believes that it is far more important for adults to share the discoveries of the young
child than it is for us to inform them of species by
name. She writes: " I sincerely believe that for the
child, and for the parent seeking to guide him, it is not
half so important to *know* as to *feel*. If facts are the
seeds that later produce knowledge and wisdom, then
the emotions and the impressions of the senses are the
fertile soil in which the seeds must grow. The years of
early childhood are the time to prepare the soil. Once
the emotions have been aroused — a sense of the beautiful, the excitement of the new and the unknown, a feeling of sympathy, pity, admiration or love — then we
wish for knowledge about the object of our emotional
response. Once found it has lasting meaning." [1]

[1] From *Help Your Child to Wonder,* by Rachel Carson. Copyright,
1956, by Rachel Carson. Used by permission.

To us who teach in home and church, this indicates that we must share the child's discovery of the mysteries of the world about him and the mystery of his very own self. In such experiences of awe and wonder we have the privilege of guiding him from feelings about God toward knowledge of him.

PRAYER

Many four- and five-year-olds have been taught to pray in their homes at mealtime and at bedtime. Some express their own ideas and others repeat memorized prayers. Some live with adults who pray with them, and others with adults who listen casually or not at all. In the church kindergarten the teacher can further the understanding of prayer as she prays with individuals or groups. Sometimes she will say the words alone, and sometimes she will ask the children to repeat them. At other times she will lead the children first in conversation as to what they will talk to God about, then will include in her prayer what each child has suggested or wishes to say.

Sometimes the teacher will make use of our heritage of prayers, or songs and poems that are prayers. In these ways children are helped to know the vocabulary of prayer so that they are not dependent upon memorized prayers. Memorized words are helpful for a unison grace, as at lunchtime in the two- or three-hour kindergarten session. They are also used in singing prayers. Whether poem or song, it is essential that the idea expressed is understandable to the child and related to the immediate experience.

The teacher will be careful to direct all prayers to God and not to Jesus who taught us to pray to God. She will use " you " rather than " thee " in addressing God so that the child is not confused and can speak naturally to him.

Meaningful prayers should be short — two or three sentences at most — and should contain one idea expressive of the situation at hand. The teacher will gradually enlarge the children's understanding of prayer by the way she guides them in thinking. Most four- and five-year-olds are thankful for people and possessions and will ask God for what they want. The teacher must help them to think deeper and guide them in understanding about God's plan for people and for his world, the reasons for sickness and accidents, our part in showing his love to other people. Rather than simply naming the people they are thankful for, the teacher may ask the questions: "What do you like to do with the people at your house? What pleasant things do they do for you?" After many have replied, she will suggest that they thank God for his plan of growing in families; then each will use his own words again but this time in prayer addressed to God in gratitude for special acts and occasions. Or she may ask, "What can you do to help your family?" Their responses can lead to prayer asking God to help them remember "that Mother needs me to empty the wastebaskets," or "Grandfather needs me to carry the newspaper upstairs to him." On another occasion she might ask: "What can you do to make it easier for Mother when you are sick? How can we help God take care of ourselves? Perhaps you planned to play outdoors and then it rains. What can you do to have a happy day in the house?"

Reverence in prayer may be felt in different postures, and children imitate the teacher. If a group of children stop in their outdoor play to look at a singing cardinal, the teacher may lead them in prayer as they look upward. If the children have stooped down to better see the wee sprouts of tulip bulbs they planted in the churchyard, they may pray as they look. In either case it would interfere with the spirit of prayer if the teacher stopped to ask that the children bow their heads and fold their hands. It is hoped that gradually the children will learn that they can speak with God anytime and anywhere, which indicates that no set position of head and hands is essential to all times of praying. But they can also be led to see why and when and how prayer in certain places and positions can be right and natural too.

As in every other part of the session, the child absorbs from the adult the real meaning of what is happening. The sincerity and reverence of the parent or teacher who is actually experiencing prayer with the child give to that experience truth and feeling. In a way the adult is sharing with the child a personal relationship to God.

USE OF THE BIBLE

Fortunate is the child who lives in a home where the Bible is used by the adults as naturally and as often as other books are used. Such a child is growing up to think of the Bible as a mighty important book! He discovers that Father and Mother depend on the Bible; they cannot get along without it. Arthur lived in such a family, but at age five he did not yet realize it. Then one Sunday his church school teacher suggested that the children ask someone at home to read them the story she had told them from the Bible. Arthur went home and hunted for a Bible. He could not find one anywhere! He went to his mother almost tearfully asking if they had a Bible in their house. " Certainly," his mother replied reassuringly. " Just run upstairs and look on the table next to Mommy's and Daddy's big bed. We keep it there because we read it together every night." This made her realize that it was time they shared this reading with Arthur too. The people Arthur cared for in both home and church were making use of the Bible as a necessary part of their common life. He was beginning to realize this fact.

The Bible is an adult book; very little of it is suitable reading matter for children in the kindergarten. But its basic message and spirit can be conveyed to them in many ways. A few stories and verses are within the kindergarten child's understanding and so can be used in home and church. But more important for him at this age is the building of positive attitudes toward the Bible. Parents and teachers want him to begin to feel eagerness and curiosity in regard to the Bible. Such attitudes are basic if we would have the child, as he grows older, increasingly seek to know what God says to him through the Bible.

The kindergarten teacher will read a short verse from her Bible, not from her curriculum material. The way she refers to the Bible and reads from it will show her love, enjoyment, and appreciation of it. She will not set the Bible up on a special table to stay there during the session as if it were an object to worship, but she will place it where she can reach it easily to use it. She may place a Bible in the book corner so that the children can sometimes handle it and hear familiar stories or verses read from it. She may read from it, too, to interpret a picture. She may place her Bible on the piano so that when the children are practicing a new song, she can open it and read the same or similar words from the Bible. She may put it on the table in the housekeeping center so that during informal play she and the children can read a prayer from it when they are playing family mealtime. Possibly her Bible will be one with a soft, pin-seal cover — a choice and different book for the children to feel and handle; it may even have a blue or red cover for the children to see and enjoy. Above all else, she herself will be using the Bible every day and growing in her understanding of God's word to her. She will read several versions and use a Bible commentary in order that she can gain new and deeper understanding. Only from her own understanding will she be able to convey joy and gratitude to her children as she uses the Bible with them.

MUSIC

Babies are full of music, in the sense of sound and rhythm. They cry and coo and gurgle before they can speak a word; they crawl and sway and teeter before they can walk a step. They respond to the human voice according to its tone of gentleness or harshness. They tap a spoon on the table and a pan on the radiator. They respond to a melody sung or played on an instrument. Before we adults realize it, children are basically involved in music. If they are neither noticed too much or rebuked, they express themselves freely and joyously in creating music.

However, as children grow older, their noises are shrill and their actions alarming to the adults who try to keep them quiet. Parents and teachers can dictate and hamper, or they can permit and even invite expression of sounds and rhythms within limits. Music can be a creative experience for children, or it can be shared with them as a finished product by adults on radio, TV, and records, and in individual performances, both vocal and instrumental. Most kindergarten children are eager for singing and rhythms. And with little or no encouragement, they will hum, glide, twirl, and make up tunes — with or without words — wherever they are and whatever they are doing.

There are several ways a parent or teacher can use music to enrich the lives of kindergarten children whether at home or at church:

By creating an atmosphere for activity, for worship, for quiet appreciation.

By inviting children to express their feelings in rhythmic movements.

By interpreting experiences through songs.

By presenting new ideas through songs.

Let us consider each of these in more detail.

First, when music creates a mood, it affects someone who is listening. Parents often sing or play quieting music after dinner in order to prepare their tired five-year-old for bedtime. Teachers in the church may use a song to unite a group of children after a busy time in individual activities. They use quieting music for rest time when the children sit relaxed or lie on their mats. They play or sing joyful music to help children express gratitude to God. They may use a singing game to develop a sense of happiness with friends. They may use beautiful listening music for sheer enjoyment. Record players are helpful in providing such listening music, and children should be taught how to manage them.

Secondly, after a work period or story time, certain music may suggest that it is time to skip and jump and whirl. This music and activity is as restful to the four- and five-year-old as the lullaby, but in a different way. It invites him to stretch his growing muscles, which are tired from being still. Sometimes children respond in motion as the music speaks to them. Other times the children may do rhythms together, such as skipping, hopping, running, and walking on tiptoe. Often when children are painting or using clay, they sway and keep time to music as they work; or they may make up a song that sings itself with their work. This occurs too when they are playing train, barnyard, or house. An alert teacher listens for such creative expressions, appreciates each one, and asks the child to share " his song " with others. Even crowded rooms will permit some of this kind of freedom and enjoyment of music through rhythmic movements.

Another way for children to enjoy music with their whole bodies is through the use of rhythm instruments. This can be in a secluded place outdoors or indoors where they may stand or sit at will, using rattles, rhythm sticks, and drums to feel the joy of keeping time. Some prefer to use their hands to clap. The melody may be sung by the teacher or played on an instrument, such as a guitar, autoharp, piano, or phonograph. Gradually the older children become interested in whether the sounds are fast or slow, loud or soft, light or heavy. Instruments for children may be homemade but should have a musical tone to be worthy of use. Good drums, sticks, tambourines, sand blocks, gongs, and wrist bells can be made.

Thirdly, experiences are often interpreted or enriched by a song that is sung spontaneously. A teacher took her children for a walk around their church one spring morning when a bird's song came clearly from a leafy tree. She stopped and listened. All the children listened. Then she sang,

> " I saw a bird in the top of a tree,
>   This is the song he was singing to me:
>   ' God loves us all in a wonderful way:
>   Be happy, be happy, today.' "

Back in their room the teacher sang it again and again, and many of the children joined her. It interpreted a lovely experience they had had together.

What teacher has not been greeted by a shiny-eyed four-year-old saying, " See my new shoes! " One friendly teacher always appreciates such happiness by singing softly to the child.

> " My shiny shoes are new you see,
>   My mother put them on for me,
>   My mother put them on for me." [1]

Fourthly, new ideas can be presented through songs. Once a group of children came to Sunday church school and discovered an entire wall had a painting on it. There were apple trees with bright red fruit, birds on their branches, rabbits, squirrels, and flowers underneath. The beauty of the rolling fields and blue sky made it a delightful picture. After conversation about God's plan for the growing things in it, the teacher sang the song,

> " Thank you for the world so sweet;
>   Thank you for the food we eat;
>   Thank you for the birds that sing;
>   Thank you, God, for everything." [2]

[1] From *Song and Play for Children,* by Danielson and Conant. Copyright, The Pilgrim Press. Used by permission. In some cases she must use " grandma " or " daddy " instead of " mother."
[2] By Edith Rutter Leatham. Used by permission of Lorna Hill.

This was a beginning for these city children to learn where food comes from and to know that God is the ultimate giver of every good gift.

Another song helped a group of children learn about the shepherds at Christmas time. They knew about Mary and Joseph and the coming of the baby Jesus. The teacher read parts of the story in the Gospel of Luke to them and with pictures interpreted the meaning of shepherds and sheep. Then she sang,

> " Shepherds leave the hillside
> And their woolly sheep.
> In a crib they find him,
> Jesus, fast asleep! " [1]

As she sang it again, the children pantomimed the action.

Picture songbooks may be kept not only on the piano but on the bookshelf or browsing table so they can be used by individual children, sometimes with a teacher. Occasionally, one or two children find a song that they wish to share with the others.

Many teachers have never thought of such uses of music to enrich the lives of the children in the church kindergarten. Instead, they use the songs they liked when they were children, those suggested by parents or heard on radio or television. Consequently, much poor music is used today and much good music is used poorly. Let us consider the following questionable practices:

The use of adult songs, with symbolic meanings. Teachers add gestures to these songs and thereby think they are childlike. There are excellent songs

[1] Used by permission of Simcoe Publishing Company.

planned distinctly for preschool children in both words and music. Search for the best so that the songs will help the children grow in understanding.

Insistence that the children sing loudly. An emphasis on loudness takes away their concentration on the words and feeling in the music as well as being a physical strain.

Dependence upon a pianist for every song. Often the pianist is a poor musician — or an improviser who embellishes with chords and runs, thereby losing the melody. A teacher who guides the children in singing a song exactly fitted to the moment, without waiting for a pianist to find the page, is using music effectively with young children.

The use of long, involved songs. A song for four- and five-year-olds should be brief — usually two to four lines with a single idea.

The use of songs with tricky music. A clear melody using only short intervals within the range of D above middle C to high E is best suited to young children; also regular time beat and only the simplest harmonization when a piano is used.

Memorizing a song line by line. A new song can be introduced first by using its tune in two or three sessions. Then the teacher sings the song to the children at a time when it has meaning. By singing it over and over again, she helps them to join her and they learn the song in its entirety.

Asking the children what songs they would " like to sing." This results in using only old-time favorites without introducing new ones. Songs should be selected and learned in accordance with the purpose of each unit and session. If a list is kept, by subject matter and by seasons, of songs learned, there will be a well-rounded supply to be used in many units of study.

A teacher or parent can depend upon the songs given by the major denominations in their curriculum materials and also in their recommended songbooks. Memorize each song before sharing it with children. Make it your own so that you can use it naturally. Some songs are really stories and can be sung by the teacher or visiting parent with no thought of teaching them to the children.

Encourage children to create songs. Be alert to recognize chants made up as they work and play. Have them share the songs with the whole group. Sometimes conversation will lead to the formation of a new verse to a song they already know.

Learn how to teach a song:

Be able to pitch it high enough if no instrument is used to start you.

Introduce the music first, playing it at several sessions simply for listening.

Sing the entire song without accompaniment at a time when it is meaningful.

Talk about its meaning; show pictures that help to interpret it; use it with a story or Scripture reading.

Sing it several times in succession, letting the children sing with you. If an instrument is used, play only the melody line.

Use it at different times in the session and on successive days.

Teach the song to parents or send a copy home so it may be sung by families.

Parents and teachers can enrich the lives of children through choice experiences with music in proportion to their own knowledge and appreciation. Listen to good music for children, such as the best phonograph records, operas by children's theater companies, creative rhythm classes. Inquire who is the best music teacher in your local schools and watch her as she leads children in listening to music, interpreting it through rhythmic movements, singing songs. Try to understand children's music; enter into the spirit of it. In the privacy of home, listen and try to feel what a child might feel — the urge to run, to hop, to slide, to crawl. Sing children's songs in the fresh spirit of childhood, as if you had just found this lovely thing. Watch for listening music that will set the tone for a snowy winter morning or a rainy, gray day, such as excerpts of classics that the children can enjoy now and recognize later as parts of longer themes. Discover how music has been a form of religious expression through the ages and how it can help you to express your own deepest thoughts and feelings.

STORYTELLING

A story is a picture painted in words. A story is music played by the human voice. Its colors and tones make a person forget himself for the time being and live the experiences he hears and visualizes. A good story, well told, is a delight to the listener who feels, thinks, and acts with the people in the story.

Stories best suited to kindergarten children are those which involve their needs and interests as given in Ch. 1. These characteristics are considered by denominational curriculum writers. When we teachers and parents add books and stories from other sources, we too must select them with thoughtful care. After rereading the chapter on the physical, mental, social, and emotional needs of four- and five-year-olds, we will realize that children are interested in things that happen right now, right here, to someone just like themselves. The sounds of the words and the lilt of the phrases add rhythm and repetition to make a fine story. Experiences of tasting, touching, hearing, smelling, and seeing — all are needful and acceptable. And, of course, a story for a group of kindergarten children is brief, with more movement than description.

Stories are used for a number of purposes at home and in the various sessions of weekday, vacation, and Sunday church school. They may be used

> *To give pleasure:* relaxing with a nonsense tale; laughing with happy people or animals.
>
> *To give information:* how the world came to be; how babies grow; how God plans for families, what Jesus said and did.
>
> *To express attitudes and feelings:* gratitude to others; gladness for friends.
>
> *To suggest a way to act:* what to do when mother is sick; how to make a guest happy.
>
> *To interpret an experience at hand:* solving group problems by weaving a story about other children so that the group sees itself objectively in the story.
>
> *To give new experiences:* how food grows (for city children); how ferryboats work (for inland children); how doctors help sick people; what moving vans do for people.
>
> *To reveal the thoughts of children:* creating from their remarks or experiences stories that are valuable for retelling.

Many stories may be told; others may be read from picture books. Some may be shared with one or two children at a time; others may be told to the entire group. In a large group stories are better told than read. Any teacher can develop a good storytelling technique if she will try to make the story come alive, first for herself and then for the children. One Sunday church school teacher worked out this plan for herself:

> On Sunday afternoon read the story that is to be told the next Sunday.
>
> Read it at least once each day that week.
>
> Visualize it, making mental pictures of the characters — what they look like, where they are, what they do, and how they feel.
>
> On Friday try telling the story aloud in a room alone, being sure to know the order or sequence of events. If it is impossible to tell it without forgetting, then restudy the introduction, climax, and conclusion.
>
> On Saturday tell it again until the story people live and breathe. Read it or tell it the last thing before falling asleep and the first thing upon awaking.
>
> On Sunday *enjoy* telling that story!

We notice that this teacher did not take time to memorize the story word for word. She let the process of reproducing it become a part of her by the constant repetition day by day of reading or thinking or telling the story. When she could actually forget herself, she knew she would be able to tell the story to the children with sincerity and beauty. She knew that she could move through the story in such a way that no child would miss its magnetic appeal.

A teacher needs to discover what happens to her facial expression as she tells stories. Practice your stories in front of a miror (devastating, but helpful). Do you frown as you speak? Are your facial muscles tight or relaxed? Do you lift your eyebrows? Such quirks are often seen on the faces of the children who watch you. If you are sensitive to them, you can discover what distracting mannerisms you may have! Your hands may help or hinder, depending on what you do with them.

As a teacher engages in more and more storytelling, she will learn to play better on her own special instrument, the human voice. When you practice alone, listen to your words for clarity. Are they distinct or fuzzy? Listen to the tone of your voice. Is it high-pitched and shrill? Try to lower it gradually so that it is deeper and more mellow, more musical in shading. Listen to your tempo. Do you tell the entire story and every story at the same rate of speed? Some sentences should go slowly and others fairly run. If it is possible for you to tell a story on a phonograph record or a tape that you can play back for your own listening, do so. You will be amazed at how you sound, and you will not believe it is yourself speaking. This is an excellent method to use for consistently improving one's speech and effectiveness in storytelling.

A good story pleases not only the children but the teacher as well. She sees their faces light up as she tells the story. She hears their discerning comments when she finishes. Or she feels their sense of awe and wonder as together they pray or sing immediately after the story. It is the combined effect of story and teller that makes the positive impression, so that the story becomes a rich experience in understanding.

Chapter 5

WAYS OF CHRISTIAN NURTURE (continued)

USE OF CREATIVE ART MATERIALS

In the history of the "Beginners' Department" or church kindergarten, "busy work" and "handwork" were terms that indicated a period when the children did the same thing at the same time, usually using crayons and sometimes paste and scissors. The work accomplished was primarily the teacher's work, for she prepared patterns for the children to color in between the lines or to cut on the lines. This over-all procedure has been encouraged by parents and grandparents who, having themselves grown up in this tradition, eagerly ask their children each Sunday, "What did you make in church school this morning?" Today the teacher of the church kindergarten wants more than busy work for her children; she wants the work done by their hands to involve also their minds and emotions.

There are many times when words are useless to the preschool child, both as he listens to them and speaks. At such times his inmost feelings and thoughts are expressed more satisfyingly in other ways, such as, finger painting, carpentry, clay manipulation, paper-tearing, or drawing. The results may not be as understandable as words to parent or teacher but, if she is wise, she does not insist upon knowing what every painting, drawing, or clay object is about. She must realize that *what happens to the child in the process of working* is more important than what he makes. He should have many opportunities to express himself through several kinds of art materials.

THE VALUES IN USING CREATIVE ART MATERIALS

Besides being a means of expression, creative art materials provide several other values. They help a child *acquire knowledge* about the things and the people in the world around him, and he discovers also his relationship to them. They *provide group experiences* in which ideas are shared, materials are used in common, work is appreciated for its individuality. In a simple activity, such as working with clay at a table with other children, the child begins to learn what a group is and what it is like to function as a responsible member of a group; living in a democracy — in a Christian community! They *encourage the solving of problems* when the parent or teacher helps the child to figure out things for himself, answer his own questions, find new ways of working. Children become aware that their memory of past experiences helps in new endeavors. Creative art materials also *offer experiences for planning, carrying out, and evaluating an undertaking*. Children need the feeling of fulfillment or completion in their work, and usually at this age they need an adult to guide them through the process. There is keen satisfaction in achievement. They *promote orderliness* — keeping supplies in certain places, cleaning up, and putting away after work is done. Materials are placed on shelves within reach of children who learn that each material is kept in its own container or place. They are taught how to wash paintbrushes, clay boards, and table tops, how to put clay away and put lids on finger-paint jars. Enough wastebaskets, dustpans, brushes, and sponges are provided so that many may work simultaneously. Finally, the use of creative art materials *gives pure pleasure* in both individual and group activities through the use of the senses — in touching, seeing, hearing, smelling.

From the traditional pattern in the Sunday church school of one kind of activity for all children at a stated time, we are moving in the direction of more freedom for a child to choose the work he will do, more variety of materials available for his choice, appreciation of his need to experiment, and appreciation of each child's development in using various materials. Parents and teachers are becoming more conscious of the value of individuality rather than conformity in personal expression. We do not compare Julia's picture or clay object with those of Jean; we accept them as hers. We make it possible for her to try many kinds of art materials and compare her work this month with her work of last month or last year to see how she is progressing. " Since every child is born with the power to create, that power should be released early and developed wisely. It may become the key to joy and wisdom and, possibly, to self-realization. . . . The awakening of the creative power is often impeded because teachers put their chief interest into helping the pupil produce a good drawing or painting." [1]

This quotation applies to parents and other adults in the home as well as to teachers, for most all of us have been guilty of unwittingly blocking this " power to cre-

[1] From *The Artist in Each of Us,* by Florence Cane. Used by permission of Pantheon Books, Inc., publishers.

ate " in our children. We have given them coloring books and shown them how to color in between the lines. This in reality was saying: " I know you cannot draw but here are some good pictures. It may be hard for you to color carefully, but keep trying and you will succeed." When they get used to these exact pictures, they know immediately that they cannot do so well, so they do not even try; they fail before they begin. Careful coloring is dependent upon muscular co-ordination, and in preschool years the muscles of fingers are not yet developed sufficiently for this difficult kind of control. In addition, coloring someone else's picture is not meaningful work of genuine worth! The child becomes discouraged, loses interest, and is unhappy. This affects his attitude toward himself and his abilities. When this negative attitude occurs in church school, it affects the child's attitude toward the church also. Instead of coloring books, patterns, or pictures to cut on the lines, the child should have large sheets of paper, big crayons, finger paints, brush paints, clay, hammer and nails. Such materials, if properly used, can provide more deep-seated pleasure throughout life than any of the commercial gadgets for making art objects.

The Teacher's Guidance

What is the teacher's part in the use of the work period of art activities? A teacher will use the suggestions in her denominational curriculum materials as creatively as she and the other teachers are ready and able to use them. She will set the stage for the children's curiosity and interest by the way she arranges the room and art materials. She will give simple directions when children use a material for the first time; then, freedom to work. After a child has experimented several times with finger paints, clay, chalk, or brush paints, he may choose to make designs or express ideas. But children need time to feel what each material is like. Gradually some form will take shape in painting or clay, and the child will name it or tell what he was thinking. Although most five-year-olds can plan their work and produce something adults can identify, neither four- nor five-year-olds should be expected to do this. They paint and name it, continue painting and rename it, and change their original purpose several times before their work is finished. The teacher will encourage or praise each child according to his need. She makes it possible for children to feel free in their work by her wholesome attitude toward the worth of their ideas and experiments. No matter what a child has done, whether he has painted a recognizable idea or daubed colors, his work is vitally important to him, and so is sharing it and learning to appreciate the work of other children.

In a weekday or vacation church school kindergarten, many creative art materials are made available to children in a long, free-choice period during which they may also choose more familiar materials. All are placed in work centers — those used for building, easel painting, clay or dough work, housekeeping, cutting-tearing-pasting, carpentry, making puzzles, reading, finger painting, using rhythm instruments, drawing. In a Sunday session of one hour, some materials are not suitable because they require too much time for their creative use and for cleaning up afterward. However, many more are suitable than are used in the average church. Much depends upon the teachers' initiative and willingness to try something new. Some teachers hope to meet the needs of their children by occasionally changing the variety of materials used on Sundays, by using others such as finger paints at frequent weekday parties where mothers assist, and by stimulating parents to provide art materials for the child at home.

The following charts give the basic requirements for several types of work.

Painting with Brushes

Materials Needed

Poster paints in screw-top jars.

One or two brushes in each jar.

Paper — Manila or newsprint in 12″ x 18″ and 18″ x 24″ sizes.

Jars of water for washing brushes.

Sponges, aprons.

Enamel paint — best for painting objects made of wood or clay. Use turpentine to clean brushes used with enamel.

Where Done

Standing at an easel, with oilcloth or papers on the floor underneath.

Standing at a low table.

Sitting on the floor — a group of four children can work on newspapers or a large rectangle of oilcloth with the paint jars between their papers.

Standing at the wall where paper is taped on and a ledge is built for paint jars, newspapers on floor.

Painting with water on chalkboards — pictures soon disappear!

Directions to the Teacher

If using powdered poster paints, mix clear, bright colors before the children arrive. Add water to powder gradually and stir smooth until consistency of light cream.

Keep paints in screw-top jars with lids on tight when not in use.

Stir paints each day before using.

Have sponges handy to wipe up spilled paint and water.

Write name on each paper — using upper right-hand corner makes each easy to locate.

Teacher's Directions to a Child

" Choose any colors you want. Pull your brush against the edge of the jar to get off extra paint. Too much paint drips! When you have finished with that color, put the brush back in the jar where it belongs."

Cleanup Necessary

Wash brushes.

Put lids on paint jars.

Clean up table, oilcloth, or newspapers — unless paintings are to be left there to dry.

Wash hands or wipe them on wet sponges or towels.

Put away aprons.

FINGER PAINTING

Materials Needed

Newspapers or oilcloth to work on.

Glazed shelf paper.

Water and sponge to moisten papers.

Aprons or smocks.

Towels or rags.

Finger paints and spoons in bowls or wide-mouthed pint jars with screw tops.

Recipe for making paint:

1½ c. laundry starch mixed with enough water to make a paste. Add

1 qt. boiling water. Cook until mixture is clear. Stir constantly and add

½ c. talcum for fragrance (may be omitted)

Let cool, then add

1½ c. soap flakes, mixing well.

Pour into jars, add

½ tbs. poster or powder paint to each jar as desired.

Where Done

Standing at low tables — use several thicknesses of newspaper or an oilcloth to protect tables.

Sitting on the floor in groups such as described under " Painting with Brushes."

Directions to the Teacher

Make paints with clear, bright colors.

Keep paints in wide-mouthed screw-top jars and cover them when not in use.

Put newspapers down; lay out sheets of glazed paper and moisten them with water.

Put bowls or jars of finger paints beside the glazed papers for easy access to each child working.

Before giving directions to a child, be sure that his smock sleeves are rolled up above the elbows.

Write name on upper right-hand corner of each painting.

See that each child helps with cleanup.

When dry, press the paintings on the wrong sides under weights or with a warm flatiron.

Teacher's Directions to a Child
"When we do finger painting, we use wet paper and thick paint like this. Choose the color you want. Put two or three spoonfuls on your paper. Put both hands in the pretty paint and spread it over the paper. The paint feels nice and squishy! "

Later you may want to add:

"Isn't it fun? You can draw with your fingers. Your fingernails can make tiny, thin lines. Your whole arm, right up to your elbows, can make big, fat lines. Finger painting is lots of fun."

Cleanup Necessary
Wash hands in lavatory or bucket of water.
Wash spoons.
Put lids on jars of paint.
Put away aprons or smocks.
Prepare a place for paintings to dry.

DRAWING WITH CRAYONS

Materials Needed
Large sheets of paper — 12″ x 18″ or 18″ x 24″, such as newsprint, Manila, or shelf paper.
Fat, kindergarten-type crayons.

Where Done
Sitting at tables or on the floor.

Directions to the Teacher
Encourage large movements. Most children have used crayons, but few have worked on paper 18″ x 24″.
Be sure names are on upper right-hand corner (or the spot you have chosen consistently).

Teacher's Directions to a Child

  " It is fun to have a big, big piece of paper to work on
    with crayons. See if you can make a picture that al-
    most fills up the paper."

  Ideas for pictures may develop during conversation
    time when planning the work.

Cleanup Necessary

  Put away crayons.

  Put drawings on tack board or other chosen spot.

DRAWING WITH COLORED CHALK

Materials Needed

  Tough wrapping or butcher paper, 12" x 18".

  Water and sponge to moisten papers.

  Newspapers to work on.

  Colored chalk sticks, 1" in diameter.

  Aprons.

Where Done

  Standing at low tables. Use several thicknesses of
    newspaper or an oilcloth to protect tables.

  Sitting on the floor in groups, such as described under
    " Painting with Brushes."

  Dry chalkwork can be done on chalkboards if avail-
    able.

Directions to the Teacher

  Put newspapers down, lay out sheets of paper, and
    moisten them with water.

  Put boxes of chalk beside papers.

  Write name in upper right-hand corner of each paint-
    ing.

  When dry, press under weights, if necessary.

Teacher's Directions to a Child
  " Choose the colors you want in your picture. Use the
    flat side of the chalk. Sometimes you may want to
    use the end of it too."

Cleanup Necessary
  Put chalk in boxes.
  Wipe hands on wet rags or towels.
  Put away aprons.
  Prepare a place for drawings to dry.

CUTTING, TEARING, PASTING

Materials Needed
  1. For Collage
     Paste and construction paper.
     Bits of colored papers cut in various odd shapes.
     Odds and ends, such as feathers, bits of cloth and
       cotton, soda straws, twigs, grasses, yarn, buttons,
       wood shavings, gummed labels.
     Scissors, stapler, a punch.
     Wet sponges or towels to wipe hands as work pro-
       ceeds.
  2. For Scrapbooks
     Scrapbook pages.
     Cutout pictures from magazines.

Where Done
  On newspapers or oilcloth.
  Sitting at tables or on the floor.

Directions to the Teacher
  1. Children can help by getting the materials from
     the cupboard if they are on low shelves and kept
     in containers easily carried.

Be sure names are on each child's work.

Arrange for a place to put pictures until taken home.

2. If you use loose-leaf scrapbook pages, each child can work at his own speed.

Choose a subject for the scrapbook that is in keeping with the curriculum unit. Collect pictures in advance on such subjects as: growing things in God's world, people helping baby animals, children helping grandparents, children helping babies, children playing together happily, Jesus at his teaching.

Write in the books related Bible passages, songs, or parts of stories the children know.

Teacher's Directions to a Child

1. " In these boxes are bits of paper and many other interesting things. They will make a pretty picture if you paste some on a paper — put them any way you wish. You may want to tear colored paper or cut it into different shapes."

2. " When we decided to make a scrapbook, what did we say it would be about? Miss Brown told us a story about _____. Look in this pile of pictures and choose one or two you think tell us how to ——, just as we heard in the story. Then you can paste the pictures on scrapbook pages."

Cleanup Necessary

Wash hands or wipe them on wet towels or sponges.

Pick up leftover materials and put them away.

Put pictures or scrapbook pages in selected place.

Pick up scraps from the floor.

CLAY AND DOUGH WORK

Materials Needed

1. Natural clay purchased in bulk, or clay powder prepared in advance so clay can mature.

   Tightly covered crock or galvanized container for clay.

   Water, with a rag or sponge to moisten working surface.

   Boards or oilcloth to work on.

2. Salt dough, instead of clay, may be used for manipulating and pounding. Recipe:

   2 c. flour, 1 c. salt, enough water to make pliable, 2 tbs. of salad oil, few drops of food coloring. Keep in cool place in plastic bag.

   Flour in a shaker and rolling pin may be used sometimes, particularly in the housekeeping center.

Where Done

Sitting or standing at tables.

Pieces of plyboard 9" x 12" are called clay boards and are used by individuals. A child can thus clean up his work when finished by putting away his clay and washing his board.

Or clay may be worked on the moistened " cloth " side or back side of oilcloth. This moisture keeps the clay from getting too dry.

Or pieces of heavy wrapping paper may be used on tables.

Directions to the Teacher

Clay must be easily pliable but not sticky. When it cracks from dryness, moisten it and knead on oilcloth back, dampened.

To keep an object, set it on a paper. Write the child's name and anything he may have told you about it. Let it dry gradually, away from direct heat; then it can be painted with poster paint and shellacked, or it can be fired in a kiln and glazed.

To keep old clay workable, put in a heavy wet cloth in a covered, galvanized bucket or in a covered crock; knead small, dry pieces into larger balls by using a little water.

To keep dough workable, put it in an airtight container in a cool place. If it gets sticky between uses, add flour.

The children may sometimes wish to make dishes for the housekeeping center, hand plaques, pencil holders, or bowls for gifts.

Teacher's Directions to a Child
" Take a lump of clay about as big as an orange or a cup. Push it — squeeze it — pound it! Doesn't it feel good? "

On occasion you may want to add: " Often you can make a piece of clay look like a ball or an apple — or almost anything you want! "

Cleanup Necessary
Roll tiny bits of clay together into balls.
Put clay and dough in their respective containers.
Wash hands or wipe them on wet sponges or towels.

CARPENTRY
Materials Needed
Claw hammer, vice, clamps, saw.
Large-headed nails of various sizes, brads, screw eyes, hinges, button molds.
Soft wood — keep a variety of pieces in a box.

Where Done
   At workbench or sturdy table.

Directions to the Teacher
   Let only a few work at a time to avoid accidents.
   Be sure child uses hammer as a tool only and does
      not swing it.
   Coat finished objects with poster paint or enamel.

Teacher's Directions to a Child
   " Have you ever used a hammer to pound nails? This
      is the way you can pound a nail to hold two boards
      together. Pound carefully so you hit the head of the
      nail — and not your finger! "

Cleanup Necessary
   Put hardware in boxes and tools in place.
   Put wood away.

ILLUSTRATIONS OF GUIDANCE

The following illustrations show how one teacher
guided her children in creative work with crayons and
paper for materials, and conversation for stimulation.
One Sunday morning her curriculum included a story of
how a brother helped his mother care for their baby. It
was used to interpret the Bible verses for that day.
When work time came, they talked together about what
this brother had done and added things that they might
do. The teacher asked: " What does baby need that you
can get for Mother? " They named blankets, powder, a
sweater, toys. " What toys does your baby like? " They
named rattles, shakers, balls.

David and Deborah decided that they would draw

toys, so they were dismissed to go to the table where crayons had been placed. David said: " I can't draw a toy. Will you show me? " The teacher replied, " Look at the ball! " David said, " I can't make it go round." " Try it," replied the teacher, making her hand go in circular motions. He tried and said, " Oh, I see! " as he started from a dot and made a solid circle larger and larger. " If you put a handle on it, you will have a rattle," suggested the teacher. David drew a handle and then added another ball at the other end. He made two such rattles. Then he said: " Now I'll make a ball — I can't make a blanket. Will you draw one for me? " " You try! A blanket is square like this," said the teacher as she again motioned with her hands. David looked at Deborah's picture and heard her tell the teacher that she was making little blocks. He said, " I can't draw blocks." " Try it! " came the teacher's encouraging voice once more. He made three blocks, then straightened up in his chair and announced, " Now I can make a baby." And he did. He was proud of his picture, which included two purple rattles, a red ball, small brown blocks, and a brown baby. It was his work indeed — better than he had imagined he could do because a wise teacher encouraged him and stimulated his thinking.

The second illustration occurred in a vacation school with five-year-olds. As part of the getting-acquainted time, each child and teacher told who lived at his house. Then they talked about their houses — the colors, the doors, the windows, the yards. They decided to draw or paint pictures of their houses, so each went to the table where the materials were that he wished to use. The next day they talked about their church, and some made pictures of it. The third day they decided to make one big picture with all their houses on it. So each cut out his own house and pasted it wherever he wanted on the long strip of wide wallpaper which was stretched out on the floor. Then they looked at the church pictures and chose one they wanted to put on the big picture. The girl who had made it gave her permission; she cut it out and pasted it in position. They looked at the picture, and the teacher said, " We need trees and flowers around our houses, don't we? " And later, " There aren't any sidewalks in front of our houses. When you come to church, don't you walk on a sidewalk? " Each child had been happy in drawing his own part; a few volunteered to draw long sidewalks going to the church, which had been put near the center of the picture, and to add the trees and flowers. On the fourth day, they hung the picture on the wall, and the teacher used it for dramatic play as she walked down the sidewalk with two fingers and stopped to knock at each door. " I wonder who lives here," she would say as she knocked. Someone always answered, and they had a conversation before she went on to the next house. The entire project was a combination of individual and group work in which the children were free to proceed in their own way and at their own speed. They all enjoyed the big picture which they had produced together and used it often during that vacation school. Occasionally something new was suggested and added.

Remembering

Children remember those things which have meaning or importance for them. They remember best what they have occasion to use often. If parents and teachers want children to really know a Bible story, a Bible verse, a song, a poem, they interpret its meaning when they first introduce it, then use it often in many different associations. Kindergarten teachers do not plan a time to "memorize" in which they drill the children on a specific song or verse, but they sing it or say it many times, in many places, in the program of the day. They relate it to dramatization, conversation, informal play, and work activities in whatever ways are suitable.

It is also true that words are remembered better if the person has a reason for remembering. Some teachers use motivations, such as these comments indicate: "Joey was absent yesterday. Let's tell him about the story we had!" "Mr. Davis is coming to visit us. Let's be sure we know our Bible verses so we can tell them all to him. This is a good time to say them together." "You will want to know this song well so that you can sing it at home for your family. Then they could learn to sing it with you." "Let's look at these pictures and remember the Bible story each one tells about. When our mothers come to visit next Sunday, they will want to hear the stories. Janice, can you tell us what is happening in this first picture?"

Children are such good mimics that they can readily imitate what an adult says. But in the church we want our children to do more than repeat words after us. So the whole process of memorizing in the kindergarten department is one of helping children understand, use, reuse, and see definite purpose in those things we want them to remember.

In most denominational curriculums, material to be memorized is built into the session plans in the ways indicated above, at times when its use is meaningful.

EXCURSIONS

Actual contacts with people and places are worth far more than talking about them. A weekday church school group in a large church got acquainted with the organist in their own room one morning. Then he asked if they would not like to see the organ and hear him play music on it. They agreed that they could do this the next day. The choir loft seemed dark and strange to them, but they felt at ease when they found a man sitting at the organ who was already a friend of theirs. He showed them the organ console and how he made music with his fingers and with his feet. Then he asked them to listen. How surprised they were to hear a song they loved to sing! So they sang as he played. They sang several songs and had a happy time. Back in their own room later that day they talked about the things they had learned and done with the organist.

Other trips in the church may be to see the furnace room, the minister's study, the kitchen, the rooms where big brothers and sisters meet, a certain stained-glass picture window — the list varies according to the type of church. In any church, the children can go with their teacher to see the pulpit Bible as she reads from it a portion that they know, or with their minister and listen as he reads from it.

Outdoor walks can be taken for various purposes: to look for signs of the season, to do work in the churchyard, to enjoy a child's swing in her yard, to search for beautiful things we wonder about, to mail a gift in the post office, to visit a shut-in, to call upon the minister in his home.

Any excursion is undertaken in accordance with the children's interests and needs. They will plan it and talk about it in advance. They will determine such rules as these: We shall go in small groups; we must stay together in each small group — no running ahead or lagging behind; all groups will wait for the others before

crossing a street. The teacher will make advance prepa-
rations also. In the illustration of the group visiting the
organist, the teacher had prearranged this trip for a day
when their curriculum dealt with learning about the
church. Some of the children had heard the church organ and others had not, so she invited the organist to
their room to tell them about it, and he in turn invited
them to go to see it the next day. Before they went they
talked about organs — what they are like, what they are
used for, how they sound. They decided to look for certain things they wished to know and to ask particular
questions of the organist. The teacher suggested that
they take their songbook and ask to have some songs
played on the organ. Later they talked about what they
had seen and heard.

Planning is necessary on both the part of the teacher
and of the children. Thus carefully done, trips are fun
and full of learning!

RESTING

Although it may hardly be thought of as a way of
teaching, rest is of such importance in the kindergarten
schedule that it is included for emphasis. Sometimes
teachers become so involved in planning a variety of
experiences that they forget to incorporate ways of resting. Rest, too, must be a learning experience. All human
beings need a balance of rest and activity in a given day.
It is important for the child to learn early about relaxation and how to enjoy it.

Fatigue must be recognized and provided for in the
kindergarten. Just as a parent can tell when his child
is tired, a teacher must also recognize when her children
need rest. Four- and five-year-olds show fatigue in a
number of ways; they laugh and speak in noisy tones;

they cry easily and fight readily; they are irritable and restless; they are unable to keep busy at tasks. In week-day kindergartens many or all of these signs are noticeable on Mondays or the day after a holiday. Teachers are aware of this and plan a simpler schedule with more rest times for such days. They are also alert to the child who has just recovered from an illness, and they make sure that he gets extra rest for several days.

Certain things that are done within the kindergarten room may cause fatigue also. If children are required to sit still for too long a time, they become restless because their growing muscles are tired and need to be used. The teacher watches the length of a story or conversation period and arranges for action, such as standing, stretching, or rhythmic movements. Such alternating of quiet and active times in itself provides rest for growing bodies. If children are surrounded by adults who talk excessively, they become tired, particularly if these adults are telling them what to do! It is far more restful to be busy in one's own way. If they are continually hurried in their work and play, children will gradually respond with irritability and crossness. Teachers and parents must examine themselves to see if they are guilty of causing fatigue in these ways.

Can resting be enjoyable to children? Or do they all resist it? The answers to both questions are dependent upon the attitudes of the adults with whom they live in home, church, and school. Rest and going to bed are often used as means of punishment. " If you aren't a good girl, I'll send you to bed." " If you can't play nicely with Susan, then you can sit on a chair by yourself." Such threats build within the minds of children the idea that resting is bad, and they will therefore have nothing to do with it until they are forced to do so. On the contrary, when an adult sits down and says: " I'm tired! I'll just sit here and rest a while. My, but this feels good! " then the child gets the idea that resting must be fun and will try it himself. The same holds true in regard to bedtime and its pleasures of rest, relaxation, and sleep.

The rest period is usually planned for the middle or latter part of the morning (and for early afternoon in an all-day session). Be certain that the children are physically comfortable for it; this means that they have gone to the toilet and have had a " lunch," such as crackers and juice, water, or milk. In a half-day session, fifteen minutes is a sufficient time for lying down, and the floor is a good place, providing there are no drafts. Some teachers use sheets of newspaper for resting mats. Others ask the children to bring a bath towel or cotton rug. These should be marked with the name or identification symbol on a specified corner. Then the child will know which one is his, which side to lie on, and at which end to put his head. When he folds it to put it away, teach him to fold it lengthwise first, to keep the head part clean, and with the identification in sight. While the children rest, the teachers should rest also. Sometimes they may begin the period by singing a quieting song or playing a record. Under dramatic play an illustration is given of the children beginning the rest period by pretending to be butterflies (page 53). The teacher sits quietly and perhaps with her eyes closed. Sometimes she may have to rub the back of a child who is tense and unable to relax immediately. She gives a signal when rest is over, such as putting up the shades, turning on the light, playing lively music, or calling each child by name, so that only a few are putting away mats at one time.

Wise teachers will evaluate the hours they spend with children in an effort to make certain they are providing needed rest in a variety of ways.

CHRISTIAN NURTURE, IN SUMMARY

Let us always be aware of the value of three things in the total process of Christian nurture. First, the necessity of using a variety of methods or ways of guiding children, as discussed in Chapters 3, 4, and 5. Some children will learn best through one method and others through a different technique. A variety of ways will appeal to all the senses and quicken the curiosity and interest we wish to keep active. We should be willing to discard old routines for improved ways.

Secondly, the necessity of finding as much space as possible for preschool children in the church. Sometimes it is only a matter of taking out some of the furniture to find more space, or rearranging the furniture to better advantage for work and play centers, or exchanging rooms with a small adult class that meets in a large room. Space extent may be improved by providing two kindergarten departments instead of one so that each group will be less crowded and there will be a better prospect for learning by the children. Churches in mild climates are using the outdoors for teaching. Space — space — and more space!

Thirdly, the necessity of finding as much time as possible. This implies that the children must feel that they have plenty of time to do this and do that, so that each one can work at his own tempo with no sense of rush. It means that the teacher provides extra things for those children who finish first so that they do not waste time dawdling or bothering others. The teacher may have only one hour with the children on Sunday but *how she uses that hour* is the important thing. The time can be stretched to one hour and a half for many who will come earlier if invited or if the teachers are ready for them. The Sunday period can be expanded by including a vacation school and, if trained leadership is available, a weekday kindergarten.

Variety, space, time — all three — go hand in hand with methods of teaching or ways of guiding children in Christian nurture.

Chapter 6

AN ENVIRONMENT THAT STIMULATES GROWTH

Current magazines dealing with interior decorating fascinate every woman who fingers their pages. They challenge her to improve her own home with beautiful colors and handy arrangements. She wants bookshelves that have interior surfaces of a contrasting color. She wants closets that have racks and hooks which automatically tell her where to put belongings. She becomes intrigued with novel " room dividers." Has she ever thought of applying such decorating ideas to church rooms and closets?

Who is responsible for the kindergarten room in the church? Does one woman control its arrangement? No, the kindergarten room is the responsibility of the governing body of the church or the committee on Christian education every bit as much as the kindergarten program. For the program makes the room and the room makes the program! So much learning from environment is possible through room furnishings and arrangement that the kindergarten room should be entrusted to many minds working seriously together to provide the best. Such a group might include the minister, the committee on Christian education, the director, and the kindergarten staff.

A room for young children is different from one for older children; adults must consider who will use each room in the church. If a room is to be used by more than one age group during the week, then the furnishings must be especially flexible but still meet the needs of each particular group. There must also be a certain room-to-room adaptability as group sizes change and shifts become necessary.

Rooms Affect People

Have you ever noticed the effect of a particular room on you? When you were invited into great Aunt Clara's parlor, you stepped carefully and sat lightly. You barely touched the antiques and cherished treasures. Everything said *do not* to you. But in her sitting room you felt free and at home in a comfortable chair with magazines to read or checkers to play. So it is that a cozy book-lined room with a contour chair invites you to enjoy books; a sunny kitchen suggests you try your favorite cake; a beautiful chapel speaks to you of great Christian concepts. Colors and furnishings literally speak to you.

Places affect children the same way; they hinder and say *do not* or they invite and say *do*. A room that hinders a child is one that is darkish and drab, where there are too many children, where muscles begging to move cannot be stretched, where there is nothing to feel and smell and do. A room that invites a child is one that is sunny, in soft colors, where a few children can sing and skip and read books as they wish, where there is something to feel and smell and do.

In thinking about a place for the kindergarten room, there are two questions to be asked: the first being, Who will use it? Boys and girls will use it who have not been away from home much, who still need the informal arrangement of homelike rooms when they begin to get acquainted with their church home. Children will use it whose muscles are growing so rapidly that they need lots of elbow room. It is more important that they have space for *moving* than chairs for sitting still. These children are hearing, seeing, smelling, tasting, feeling, reaching out to explore everything around them. Put into any new place, they are like dry sponges laid in a basin of water — they absorb their environment and it becomes a part of them.

The second question is, For what purpose do children come here? Parents, teachers, and other adults hope they will become aware of God's love as revealed in Jesus Christ, that they will grow in loving him and in living in love with one another. We realize the complexity of this brief statement. And because it *is* complex, it means that the kindergarten room and its varied equipment must be thoughtfully prepared so that nurture toward these purposes may be carried on. They suggest hard work to be done — not baby-sitting or busy work to fill the hours of children.

When we watch gardeners, we notice that they use space wisely. They would not dream of putting seedlings close together just because they are tiny and take up little space. Nor would they set out seedlings in hard, unprepared ground. They carefully cultivate the earth, add the right kind of nutrients, then set out the wee plants far enough apart to allow them to become the mature plants of their dreams. The same is true with children in the church. Just because they are small, we dare not crowd them together or put them in a barren place. We must give them ample space so that growing bodies, minds, and spirits can mature into the adults of our dreams. We must give them materials for work and play that will provide the foodstuff for such growth.

USING THE SPACE AVAILABLE

As you think of the place in your church where kindergarten children meet on Sunday, are you satisfied with it from these viewpoints?

> Is it really suited to the needs of four- and five-year-olds?
> Is it crowded with too many children?
> Does it have adequate work and play materials?
> Does it help children in Christian understanding?

If you work in a one- or two-room church and have a corner of the sanctuary for your five children, it is just as possible to make it a growing place for them as if you had an entire room. Perhaps you use the choir loft and replace the adult chairs with children's equipment during the church school hour. Drop-leaf shelves serve as tables for work. Or perhaps you use the open space in front of the first pew. Some teachers of one-room churches have made portable cupboards for their kindergarten materials by using wooden boxes and painting or staining them the exact shade of the church woodwork or walls. Here they keep books and toys, papers and crayons, and scissors. During the church service the cupboards are stored under a pew or turned with the open side against the wall. Other teachers put oilcloth covers on the pews so that children can use them as tables for pasting, painting, or clay work. They have simulated a housekeeping center by laying on the pews pieces of cloth on which are drawn a doll's bed, a tea table, a stove top; and the children live out family experiences by using them. Such ideas are creative and flexible as well as being especially helpful to children.

If you work in a basement or social hall, it is equally important to have furnishings that are attractive and clean yet can be easily put away during the week. The first requirement is movable partitions to separate the kindergarten from both nursery and primary children. The second is an arrangement for storing materials during the week. As you read further in this chapter, try to visualize how adults in your church can make proper equipment for interest corners, securing descriptive books (pages 191–192) to help you.

Perhaps you are in a large church that needs to clean out an accumulation of useless furniture in order to make the kindergarten room suitable for children's use. Or you may be in a crowded church that is looking forward to building new rooms. Regardless of the situation in which you find yourself, you have to do your own thinking in respect to it. Keep the characteristics of four- and five-year-olds (Ch. 1) uppermost in your mind and then be original in finding ways to meet their needs. Seek advice from professional children's workers in your denomination. All problems *can* be solved! They may call for imagination and patience, but they *are* surmountable.

REQUIREMENTS FOR A GOOD KINDERGARTEN ROOM

Now let us look at what is considered essential today for an ideal kindergarten room in the church. The actual space needed for an individual child's growth within a group is 25 to 35 square feet (30 is considered fair, and less than 25, poor) of floor space per child. This means that ten children will need a room approximately 12 x 20 feet in size to provide the minimum space. Some new churches have built rooms by this standard, but others find it financially prohibitive. They build the largest possible, then use creative imagination to furnish the room sufficiently without cluttering it. A rectangular room in the proportion of 3 to 4 feet lends itself best to this age group, although some leaders prefer a square room. If a church has a room that is much too small for the number meeting in it, then the group should be divided into two kindergartens, which would use the room at different hours. Sometimes rearrangement of furniture or removal of excess chairs and tables will give more space. If the floor is warm, it is not necessary to have a chair for every child. Some churches find adequate space for the kindergarten by examining all of their rooms to see if they are being used to the best advantage; a dozen adults may be meeting in a large room that might better be used for children.

If the church invites young children to its buildings, then it must do everything possible to insure their physical well-being while there. In addition to being large enough, the kindergarten room should be easily accessible to children. If at all possible, it should have its own outdoor entrance and be situated on the ground level or first floor. This provides for order and calmness in entering and leaving the room. Overstimulation and fears sometimes develop when children must use crowded corridors or stairways. It is best to have a southern exposure for warmth and sunshine, with windows that permit adequate ventilation without drafts. Although many churches have stained-glass windows, newer buildings have clear glass, particularly when overlooking a lawn or trees. Such windows are large and low so that children can look out easily and feel that the out of doors with its birds, snow, or sprouting bulbs is a part of their very room. In good weather the out of doors is used for part of the Sunday session. Going outdoors is a daily necessity in a weekday or vacation school kindergarten.

Special attention should be given to the floor covering since four- and five-year-olds spend much of their time working or playing on the floor. It should be clean, warm, and comfortable. Linoleum, tiles of rubber, asphalt, or vinyl are good for such a floor, with some washable rugs for resting or storytimes. An acoustical ceiling softens the sound of the essential noise of good work and play. It is also advisable to have toilet facilities adjoining the room. Besides the regular child-size fixtures, it is helpful to include a deep, low sink where vases can be filled, toys can be washed, and if used for weekday sessions, water play can be enjoyed.

Because a warm, clean floor is so useful in the kindergarten room, it is not necessary to have a chair for every child, but some are needed. They should be sturdy, posture chairs with the seat 10″ or 12″ from the floor and so constructed that they stack readily. This is important if the room is to be used by another group during the week. Tables to go with the chairs are 10″ higher than the seat of the chairs and the best sizes are 24″ x 36″ or 30″ x 36″. When longer tables are needed, two or three can be placed together. These smaller tables are good for a variety of purposes and are easily moved about during the session. One can be arranged for puzzles, another for clay, another for the cut-tear-paste work. The 30″ x 36″ table permits space in the center for paint and paste jars between the papers of children on opposite sides, since the usual size of paper for kindergarten drawing and painting is 12″ x 18″.

Low coat hooks make it possible for children to hang

up their own wraps. It is important to protect children's eyes, however, and this can be done by building a 10″ shelf about 3″ above the hooks. Such a shelf is also useful for hats, mittens, and pocketbooks. If space and finances permit, it is best to build cubbyholes so each child can have his own labeled place for his possessions. Such a locker will hold boots and drawings and other things brought to the kindergarten. Teachers who do not have cubbyholes for their children often use spring-type clothespins to hold together rubbers or boots, mittens, or completed work, and each clothespin is labeled with names of the children or with a flower or animal sticker chosen as a personal symbol.

In new buildings one side of the kindergarten room should be a solid wall not interrupted by windows, doors, or cupboards. This provides a unit of space for pictures, a place to put offering money or envelopes, a table for things needed by the leading teacher — especially her Bible. In such a room at group time the children will not have to face the light of windows or the movement of doors. In old buildings some teachers achieve the effect of a solid wall by hanging a neutral-colored drapery over unused doors and windows. Care should be taken to provide adequate artificial light where necessary.

In and through all of these requirements for the room is the essential element, color. Colors affect people in different ways. Children's rooms should be rich and warm in the color tones of rose, peach, or yellow where the natural light in the room is subdued. If the exposure and clear-glass windowpanes give the room strong light, then the decorating colors can be greens or blues. One key color in the same or different shades may be carried out in floor, walls, ceiling, woodwork, and furniture to give a feeling of rest and unity to the whole. Or one contrasting but complementary color may be used for furniture and curtains (if they are needed). Dark-brown floors and furniture are not necessary in these days when lovely colors are so generally used.

MATERIALS THAT WILL STIMULATE THINKING AND ACTION

Along with space and color, light and ventilation, an impression is made on the child by the materials he finds in the room. They will say to him, " don't " or " do." A good room will literally sing out to him:

> Come and see!
> Feel, hear, and smell.
> Try this —
> Work at that —
> You can do many things
> That are fun.
> It's good to have you here.

Children need materials that encourage them to work at the kind of living they observe in their homes and communities. Through their imitation of adults they feel important and they learn something about both individual and co-operative work. They try out some of the work of being a father or a mother in the housekeeping center. They are workmen when they load and drive a truck or deliver the mail. Such creative work can only occur when the environment provides stimulating materials for them to use at home or church. These materials should be kept on low, open shelves or easily accessible cupboards so the children can wait on themselves and later put things away where they can find them another time.

The following is a list of suggested materials for work centers in a church kindergarten. Items should be provided in reasonable quantity and kept clean and in good repair.

HOUSEKEEPING CENTER

washable dolls (not all the same skin color)
a few doll clothes (manageable by the children)
clothesline and clothespins
a doll crib and carriage — with bedding for each
tea table and chairs
cupboard with dishes, pans, egg beater
simple sink and stove arrangements
a flatiron (not electric) and an ironing board (not folding)
broom and dustpan
grown-up clothing: aprons, hats, gloves — for both men and women
baskets, shopping bags, pocketbooks, wallets
a telephone

BUILDING CENTER

Smooth boards and sheets of cardboard
Cardboard boxes
Blocks: hollow blocks of sturdy cardboard or wood
solid blocks that interlock
solid blocks known as "nursery school building blocks"

The latter are essential in a kindergarten department and may be purchased from school supply houses or may be made in a home workshop.

Required features: medium-weight woods, such as pine, fir, or poplar, beveled corners and edges, a coating of shellac. Use two-by-four lumber to make these sizes:

a. A square block
b. Twice as long as *a*
c. Four times as long as *a*
d. Diagonals of *a, b,* and *c*
e. Horizontals of *a, b,* and *c* (half thickness)
f. Pillars: 1½″ diameter rounds and 3″ diameter rounds cut the length of *b*
g. Triangles, curves, arches, ramps, and switches — may be made as desired

In making a set of these solid building blocks, figure on thirty blocks per child and let sizes *a, b,* and *c* comprise three fourths of the total. Take into account the approximate number of children who play with blocks at a given time.

Transportation toys, as cars, trucks, trains, buses, boats, planes. Select types that are related to curriculum purposes, such as a milk truck, moving van, dump truck, farm tractor, and trailer. Avoid windup toys.

Figurines: people — a family, several community workers; animals — of home and farm

Figurines may be purchased at school supply houses or may be made in a home workshop. For wooden figures use a jigsaw and make them of wood thick enough to permit them to stand alone. Details can be drawn or painted on the figures. Other figures can be made by reinforcing a cutout magazine picture with cardboard and tacking it to a block of wood to permit it to stand alone.

Book Corner

A Bible

Picture books related to the curriculum units on such
subjects as: home and family life, new babies, growing, grandparents, wonder in the world of nature,
foods and where they come from, families at
church, friends who help, community workers,
friends from other lands. Both pictures and reading
matter should be carefully appraised before a book
is placed in the church kindergarten.

A table, shelves, or bookrack for keeping the books

Chairs

Table-Work Center

Puzzles — educational puzzles are graded by the number of pieces according to the age of the children
using them. They have sturdy box frames or trays
and are available in a number of subjects which
should be chosen on the basis of relationship to curriculum units, just as picture books are chosen. May
be purchased from school supply houses.

Clay or dough — clean, easily malleable, and in ample
quantity, to be pushed, pounded, pressed, and
molded at will. Sometimes the dough is used in the
housekeeping center for kitchen work. For use and
types see pages 92–93.

Papers, paste, scissors, crayons, stapler, punch — for
creative pleasure. For use and types see pages
90–91.

Music Center

A good piano — if there is not sufficient space for one, a
kindergarten can get along without it providing
the teacher sings easily and often. Since melody is

of prime importance, some teachers use a simple string instrument such as an autoharp.

A record player — for songs, rhythms, resting.

Rhythm instruments — commercial or homemade.

MISCELLANEOUS EQUIPMENT

Picture File. If it is easily accessible, the children can help the teachers get out pictures.

Wonder Table. (Or this may be a shallow box or a tray) — a place to hold the treasures children bring from God's wonderful world. A magnifying glass adds to the wonder and enjoyment.

Tack Board. A good place for displaying the children's work. It may be fiberboard on the walls at the eye level of the children or a cloth tacked on the back of the piano. Sometimes a rope or wire is used, and the papers are clipped to it with clothespins.

Vases and Large Flower Frogs for Arranging Flowers. A pitcher of water will suffice if a faucet is not available. A sponge is useful for cleaning up. Children take responsibility for making their room lovely.

Growing Things. Plants give beauty and also require care that will make children aware of their growth. Pets — canaries, turtles, fish, and others — are often kept in a kindergarten that meets daily or are brought for Sunday session.

Paints and Brushes for easel painting or finger painting (for details see Ch. 5).

Workbench for carpentry, with wood and accessories (see Ch. 5) will interest girls as well as boys.

All of these materials stimulate children to choose, experiment, achieve, appreciate, and enjoy, but not all of them are essential for every Sunday church school.

Weekday kindergartens find that they need all these things and more in order to challenge children to experiment with a wide variety of materials. Environment *does* affect the growth of children.

ARRANGEMENT MAKES A DIFFERENCE

Even if a kindergarten room had these interesting things in it, there would be no guarantee that good learning would take place. First of all, how are they arranged? The teacher needs to arrange the work centers in such a way that each will help and not hinder the other. For instance, painting easel needs to be away from the blocks and trucks. The housekeeping center should have a suggestion of walls to give it partial seclusion, such as is felt by the angles of a deep-set bay window, by the way the low storage shelves for the kitchen or bedroom are placed, by the " room " partially made when the piano is placed at right angles to a wall (done only if the piano is topple-proof!). The book table should not be near the block corner or the clay table, because in these areas there is more " essential noise." Materials for arranging flowers can be picked up and put away after the children have used them, so this activity takes up space only temporarily on a table.

A second thing to be remembered in arrangement is the use of space in order to give the *feeling* of space rather than closeness or clutter. For this reason, most kindergarten teachers prefer to have a rug for group-time instead of having a chair for each child, because chairs clutter up the valuable and limited space. Organized shelves with materials neatly arranged give the feeling of space. Things that are clean and in good repair also give this feeling because there are no soiled blotches or ragged ends. Children need to feel as much wideness as possible in their rooms, for space provides freedom to move and stretch, to work and sing.

Thirdly, if the room is arranged for the benefit of those who use it, things must be on their eye level. Kneel at the entrance of your room and try to look at everything in it through the eyes and mind of a child. Are pictures too high to see? Is adult furniture in the way? Does something interesting catch your eye immediately — like a red truck on a low shelf or a doll at the tea table? Do you find a hook for your coat, a shelf for your hat, or a cubbyhole all your own for both? Where do you put your offering money or envelope when you first arrive? Surely not at the door! Does this room have a Bible — or more than one — ready for use by the teacher, or is the Bible set apart on an altar arrangement to stay there for viewing only?

CONVENIENCES FOR THE TEACHERS

So much for what the child may find in the kindergarten room if adults have selected and arranged equipment and materials with care. Now how about the teachers? What do they need? To expect children to be at home in this room means that the teachers should enjoy living here too. So there must be a place to put coats, hats, and pocketbooks neatly out of the way. There must be a teachers' cupboard which will hold the curriculum materials, teachers' guidance books on kindergarten work in the church, a picture file, and a supply of various kinds of paper. Here too are kept disposable tissues for handkerchiefs, handy bandages for scratches, pins, thumbtacks, cellophane and masking tape, and a score of other things as they are needed. Department records are kept in this cupboard also, since a desk for a secretary is not necessary in the kindergarten

room. The only adult furniture needed is a few chairs
for parents or other visitors.

THE "PLUS" OF THE KINDERGARTEN ROOM

Whether the kindergarten meets in a small corner or
a large room, whether there are five children with one
teacher or twenty with four teachers, the most important element of the place where they meet is the atmosphere — the climate. If this place in the church is
going to captivate children in learning love of God and
love of man, the teachers must live in that spirit. They
must speak and act in such a way that each child will
feel:

> This is my church.
> I am free to try many things here.
> I can work alone.
> Or I can work with other children.
> Grownups too will work and play with me.
> Grownups here love me, and they tell me that God
>   loves me too.
> This is my church.

Adults who are the most skillful in expressing Christian love and trust and joy should be chosen to work in
this place with kindergarten children. Then and only
then will the church space provided for four- and five-
year-olds take on special meaning for them. Beyond its
equipment and appearance, children will feel love as
expressed in word and action, patience as manifested
in controlled tempers and gentle words, justice as shown
in fairness and honesty, joy as evidenced in individual
friendships. The " plus " of the kindergarten room comes
through the spirit of the adults who live and work there
with one another and with the children.

Chapter 7

A SUNDAY SESSION

Like many others, Second Church had so many children in its Sunday church school that it had to rearrange rooms and schedules. The kindergarten of fifty-six children met in the department room originally built for primary children. It was a beautiful, large room with five small classrooms along one side, a toilet, an entrance to the hall, and an outdoor entrance. But even the ample space did not make it the best place for fifty-six children of ages four and five. The teachers realized that some of the children felt lost and even frightened in such a large group. They knew that it was not possible for a four- or five-year-old to be at ease and ready to learn when he was with so many children. So they discussed what they might do and decided to divide the group into a four-year-old kindergarten and a five-year-old kindergarten. They divided the large room in half with sturdy screens faced on both sides with wallboard. One group had two and the other three of the small rooms — not to use as classrooms but as centers for activity. Each group had its own entrance and both had access to the child-size toilet.

A Visit to a Kindergarten Department

Let us visit the four-year-old group on a brisk autumn Sunday. Mrs. Clark and Mrs. Lynn were there early to make sure that the room was ready and attractive. They arranged the dolls in carriage and crib, the dishes in the small cupboard, so that the housekeeping center in the bay window would be inviting. They talked about Donald who had had a birthday that past week. During the morning they opened certain windows to permit ventilation without drafts. They took the lids off the paint jars at the easel, making sure there was enough in each jar as they stirred the paint. One of the small rooms was now the block-building room. It had low shelves for blocks, trucks, and wooden stand-up figures of people and domestic animals, a wallboard for pictures, and one or two low chairs. The other small room was now the book room with a table and chairs, a case to hold books and puzzles, and a wallboard for pictures.

Mrs. Lynn was the leading teacher this month, so she had come to the church during the week to arrange pictures on the large space provided by the big screens that separated the four-year-olds from the fives. She had chosen certain pictures in keeping with the curriculum unit entitled " We Say Thank You to God." The first two Sundays of this unit were based on the themes " God Cares About Us Through Our Families " and " God Cares About Us by Planning for Food to Grow." Today's theme would be " We Show That We Care for Others When We Help Them and Share with Them." So today she added several pictures of children sharing with one another and helping grownups. Last week the department had decided that today they would bring apples to show their love and friendship to some children living together in a different kind of family — a very large number of children taken care of by some good friends, because both their mothers and fathers were at work during the day. Notes had been sent home telling about this giving project. So today Mrs. Lynn had brought a basket for their gifts, and she put it by the bulletin board under last Sunday's pictures of apples growing on trees and farmers preparing them for market. She checked to be sure that the offering basket and Bible were on a low cupboard shelf where a child could reach them.

The teachers were almost ready when Mrs. Hill arrived with Stephen. She helped every Sunday in whatever way had been planned by the teaching team. This month she would be in charge of the book and puzzle room for the opening informal period, guiding the thinking and conversation of the children along the lines of the day's theme.

" Good morning, Stephen," said Mrs. Lynn.

Stephen smiled and held up a bright yellow apple.

" You remembered to bring a gift! " replied Mrs. Lynn. " So did I and so did Mrs. Clark. There is the basket for our apples. Would you like to put yours in it? "

Stephen put his apple in the basket, then began to remove his wraps.

" Help me take off my coat, Mommy," he said, as he stood beside his mother.

" I'll help get the buttons out of the buttonholes, Stephen. But I think you can do the rest," she replied, as she encouraged him to help care for himself.

Several children arrived. Mrs. Hill watched for an opportunity to ask one of them if he would like to help get the room ready for today by placing the offering basket on the low table near the picture rail. She sat near this table so she could talk with each child or group of children, as they put their envelopes or money into the basket, about their gifts and what they would be used for.

Other children began to come. Mrs. Lynn and Mrs. Clark sat on low chairs near the entrance to greet the children. (They had discovered that when they were on the eye level of the children, they could speak to them more easily.) One child brought small yellow chrysanthemums; she knew how to fix them in a vase because she had done it before with a teacher's help. Another brought gourds for the wonder table.

As children arrived, most of their conversation was about the apples they had brought: the colors, how nice they smell, where to put them, to whom they were to be sent, how good they would taste, how happy the children would be to know about the friends who sent them. Each child's gift was appreciated individually. The teachers had put their apples on a table so that when a child came who did not remember his gift, he was asked if he would like to put one of the teachers' apples in the basket for her.

After putting his apple gift and money gift in the places provided and hanging up his wraps, each child went to the center where he chose to work. Usually a teacher helped him by asking, " Where do you choose to work first this morning? " This question aided him in making a choice and setting out to do something, rather than engaging in indefinite rambling. Many children knew immediately what they wanted to do; others needed this help in deciding. Some few children sat and looked at the others.

Mrs. Clark watched the housekeeping center from where she sat by the door. Mary and Helen went directly to the crib to get the baby dolls. Deborah put two large rag dolls on the chairs at the tea table and proceeded to cook dinner for them. Charles went to the ironing board as he had done for six previous Sundays and ironed a doll's dress. When most of the children had arrived, Mrs. Clark left her chair at the entrance and went to sit near the housekeeping center. Later when some of the children were setting the table for dinner, she showed them some cutout magazine pictures of food. They talked together about how the tomato juice might taste, and the yellow carrots and the prune salad. Then they talked about dinner and played that they were having one.

Finally, Mrs. Clark said: " I am thinking of something that my family will do before we eat dinner today. Do you do something at your house before you eat? "

" Pray," " Wash our hands," " Thank God," came the answers to her question.

" Yes, we wash our hands too, Randy, but I was thinking of praying — of thanking God for our good food just as the children in that picture are doing." She pointed to the picture on the wall beside the dish cupboard. Then she said, " At my house we sometimes pray by reading this prayer from our Bible." Mrs. Clark opened her Bible to *Ps. 75:1* and read, " We give thanks to thee, O God; we give thanks."

" We have a different prayer at our house," said Paul.

" We never have a prayer," said John.

" We do! " echoed Susan and Craig.

" As I read the Bible prayer again," said Mrs. Clark, " will you say it with me before we eat our dinner? "

Meanwhile, in the small room now used for books and puzzles, Candice and Meg were looking at the open books on the table. Early in the morning Mrs. Hill had set out a few books and puzzles. She had chosen those that were related to the curriculum unit and today's theme. She laid one book open on the table; another she opened and stood up so that the picture would catch the eye of a child as he entered this little room. Some boys were working on the farm puzzles that were on the table. When the time came that she could leave her chair by the offering basket, Mrs. Hill went into the book room. She watched for an opportunity to talk about food with these children. They looked at a book showing how bread comes from grain. They looked at the puzzles the boys had made of the dairy farm and helpers on the farm. She asked, " Who plans for food to grow so people can have such good things to eat? " They talked about farmers and God's plan for growing things, and Mrs. Hill read from the storybook, " Thank you, God," and from her Bible, *Ps. 75:1*, " We give thanks to thee, O God; we give thanks." The children talked with her about thanking God, people who help God, and how children can help.

Several children were in the block-building room that Mrs. Lynn supervised. She kept an eye and ear on the children there and occasionally had to help Chuck and Tommy understand that the blocks belonged to all the children and each must have a share. These two were older fours and built with such speed and authority that the younger children were overcome by their dominance and could not get many blocks. Mrs. Lynn talked about farms and interested some in building a fence for the animal figurines. Then she went to the wallboard to ask questions of those who were looking at the pictures. As leading teacher, she kept alert to all that was happening in the department. She watched Donald as he flitted around from place to place without engaging in any activity. She was ready to interest David in block-building when his eyes filled with temporary tears as his father left the room. Right behind her she heard Barbara start to cry and saw Johnny facing her belligerently. "What happened here?" she asked. "He hit me!" sobbed Barbara. Johnny spoke up, "She took my broom, so I socked her." Mrs. Lynn stooped down to speak to them so each could hear her clearly: "We do not take the broom without asking. We do not sock anyone. What do we do when we want a turn using the broom, Barbara?" And later, "What might you have said to Barbara when she took the broom, Johnny?" She noticed that Betsy at the easel was using too much paint, and it ran down the picture in streaks; she reminded her of how to pull her brush along the edge of the jar in order to have just the right amount of paint. Mrs. Lynn saw Helen peeking around at the five-year-olds on the other side of the screen. She walked over and watched with her, and they talked about all the things those children were doing. Then she interested Jane in taking a doll for a ride in the carriage. Meanwhile, she kept her eye on the children who were cutting and pasting, coloring and stapling.

The mother who was helping with records had arrived. She was marking the absences on a list of names posted high on the screen wallboard near the cupboard. Then she set out the crayons, paste, and papers that would be needed for an activity later in the hour. She also acted as chairman of the parents' committee which helped the teachers by collecting certain kinds of magazine pictures and preparing other materials when needed. Today she had brought the Bible verses that a mother had typed on 9" x 12" sheets of Manila paper.

All of this happened in the first thirty minutes of the

session. Then Mrs. Lynn went to each center saying, " It is almost time to put away our books " (or puzzles, blocks, dishes, dolls, etc.). Shortly she went back to each group and said: " Now it is time to put away our things. It is cleanup time." Some children began immediately; some ignored the signal; and others left their things for someone else to pick up. All this was observed by the teachers, who tried to help each child learn to put away his work or play materials. They worked *with* the children, not just to set an example but to express such ideas as: " It's good to work together," " It's fun to clean up our room," and " You are doing a fine job today." In the housekeeping corner, Mrs. Clark was singing softly to the children with whom she worked,

> " When we help each other work,
> When we help each other play,
> We will all be friends together
> And have a happy day." [1]

As the children in each center finished their cleanup work, they gathered around Mrs. Lynn who was standing in the open space on the green rug ready to play " apple seed " with the first comers. She held an accordion booklet like the ones several children had made the previous Sunday. When all the children had gathered, she said: " Billy and Chuck were absent last Sunday. Let's show them what we made and tell them about it. What kind of seed is this on the first page? And why did you color brown all around it? After the apple seed is planted in the brown earth, what does it need to help it grow? Yes, the warm sunshine and the rain. Here is the

[1] From *Kindergarten Leader's Guide, Year 1,* by Kathrene McL. Tobey. Copyright, 1955, by W. L. Jenkins. Westminster Vacation Church School Series, The Westminster Press.

sun on this page, and next, the rain. God plans for the sunshine and the rain. Then gradually the seed grows — it becomes a little green sprout. It reaches higher and higher until it becomes an apple tree. Big branches grow out with pretty blossoms and leaves. Through the summer the apple tree grows and grows. Finally, after a long, long time, apples grow on its branches like these in this picture on the last page of the booklet."

"Let's play we're apple seeds again," suggested Tommy.

"All right," replied Mrs. Lynn, and all the children got down on the rug. She repeated the story they had just reviewed about the seed. They "grew up" into trees with apples in their branches. After playing it twice, Mrs. Lynn sat down by the basket of apples and asked the children to sit on the rug with her. She said: "God cares about us. God loves us. He plans for trees to grow in the warm brown earth so that we will have apples to eat. And he plans for many other kinds of food, like . . ."

"Oranges," "bread," "prunes," said several children.

"God cares about us. So he plans for us to live in families, to love one another, to help one another. He gives us friends. And he helps us to be friends.

"Today we have brought apples to give to some other children to show them we are their friends and we love them. Let's write a letter to send with our basket of apples. What could we say in a letter to them?" Mrs. Lynn wrote with a black crayon on a large sheet of Manila paper as the children's ideas developed.

Dear Children:
　　Here are some apples for you.
　　We are sending them to tell you that we love you.

God loves us all.
He plans for apples to grow.
From the
Four-year-old Kindergarten
of the Second Church

Part of the time it was hard to talk because of the piano music of the five-year-olds in the other half of the room (there was no piano on the four-year-old side). At the end of the writing of the letter the fives began to sing " Thank You for the World So Sweet." Mrs. Lynn looked up and said: " Let's listen! Hear the song the five-year-olds are singing! " They sat intently, and then she said: " Wasn't that beautiful? They sang to thank God for the world so sweet and for the food we eat! "

" And the birds that sing," added Deborah. " I know that song. My mommy and daddy sing it to me."

" Our letter and gift of apples reminds me of a song we know." Mrs. Lynn began singing " Friends! Friends! Friends! " and the children joined her. Then she said: " Today we have a friend in our room who just had a birthday. Donald was four years old yesterday. Donald, will you stand over here by me while we sing to you? "

They sang together:

" Birthday child, to you we sing —
Happy birthday greeting! " [2]

Then Mrs. Lynn said: " We are glad you had a birthday and are four years old, Donald. God helps you to grow. Let's thank him for his loving care." With her arm around Donald, she prayed: " Dear God, thank you for helping Donald grow to be four years old. Thank you for your love. Amen."

[2] From *Song and Play for Children,* by Danielson and Conant. Copyright, The Pilgrim Press. Used by permission.

Mary volunteered that it was her birthday too, and then Helen added hers. But Mrs. Lynn said: " Our birthday chart tells us that Donald is the only one in our kindergarten who had a birthday this week. It will tell us when your birthday comes, Mary, and yours, too, Helen. All of us have birthdays. God helps us all to grow, and he loves us all." Then she stood up and began singing the song:

> " Every morning seems to say,
> ' There's something happy on the way,
>   And God sends love to you! ' " [3]

The children stood also and sang the song joyfully two or three times.

Mrs. Lynn opened her Bible and read *I Peter* 5:7, " God cares about you." She and the children said the words together. They walked across the rug to the place where today's picture was hanging on the bulletin board. " Let's sit down here by this picture. It shows a family who lived long, long ago. Mrs. Clark will tell us a story about them." Quickly but quietly Mrs. Clark changed places with Mrs. Lynn and sat on a low chair by the picture. The children sat on the rug. The story told about harvest time and how the family gave thanks to God for food. At the close she prayed: " Thank you, God, for planning for food to grow. Thank you for people who help us. Show us how to be friends and helpers too. Amen.

" Here is a picture of the family in the story. Can you tell me what they said when they prayed before eating their dinner? "

[3] Copyright, 1911, by Charles Scribner's Sons; 1939, by Tertius van Dyke; used by permission of the publishers.

"Thank you, God!" a child said quickly, and it was repeated by others.

"Yes, but in the story they said it a certain way. Perhaps someone who played in the housekeeping center this morning could remember. Mary, Deborah, or Charles — do you remember the prayer I read to you when you played make-believe dinner? Say it with me now while I read it from the Bible: 'We give thanks to thee, O God; we give thanks.'"

She led the children in saying it several times and suggested it would be good to say this prayer at home. "To help you remember it, we have typed it on a sheet of paper for you to take home. Do you want to draw pictures of food you like around the words? Or would you rather find pictures in our file to paste? She showed them a paper with the typewritten verse and how, when folded in half, it would stand up like a tent on the table. Most of the children went to places to work at the table or on the floor, and each teacher supervised a group; others went to the building center. The teachers put each child's name on his sheet. Because Donald was not interested in drawing or pasting, he took his sheet home without any pictures and spent the time watching others as he wandered from group to group.

When this work was finished and materials were put away, Mrs. Lynn called the children together on the rug. They reviewed why they had brought gifts of apples — why God plans for food and homes — ways they can thank him. They said the Bible verse together and had a closing prayer.

While the children put on their wraps, Mrs. Lynn and Mrs. Clark sat on their low chairs by the entrances so they could help some with buttons and zippers, say good-by to each one, and visit with the children before they were called for by older persons.

Mrs. Hill and the other helping mother put away extra work materials as the twenty-four children left. When alone the teachers discussed interesting things that happened with their children in the various centers early in the morning. Mrs. Lynn observed that Donald had not yet settled down to an activity. He was still watching everyone and going from group to group. Then she reminded the others about their responsibilities for next Sunday and promised to phone them early in the week to go over detailed plans.

WHAT HAPPENED IN THIS ROOM?

As you sat in the kindergarten room with these four-year-olds, how well did you observe and understand what was happening? You probably noted certain things that you would have done differently. You also felt that you would have done one part better and another part not nearly so well. But we find basic things that all wise kindergarten teachers should be doing.

The teachers arrived before any children came.

The room was one that said to children, " Try this! " " Do that! " " Come and see! " The leading teacher had done some work on the room during the week, but she also left some things to be done by the children and other teachers. This room belonged to everyone!

The children were free to choose what they wanted to do for part of the session.

Pictures, books, and puzzles were selected in accordance with the day's theme and purpose.

Every teacher was prepared to do her part.

Every child was treated as an individual person, an

important friend; the teachers spoke to each one by name.

A Bible was used at several times and places.

Attendance was recorded on the bulletin board so that the teachers could readily see who was absent and be alert to contact parents after a child was absent one or two Sundays.

The children's responsibility for their room and work materials was being developed through the careful use of cleanup time.

Last Sunday's work was related to this Sunday's by recalling specific things to tell two children who had been absent and also by acting out the ideas.

The children were not required to sit still for long periods: they stood, sat down, walked to another part of the room, sat down again. Quiet times alternated with active times.

Use of the offering money was discussed with a few children at a time as they placed their money in the container for it.

The children had an experience of giving a tangible gift — one that they liked and enjoyed. Their giving was interpreted by conversation and writing a letter so that they were led to think of loving as the meaning of giving.

A birthday was recognized in a thought-provoking way which spoke to the child on behalf of the church. It was done differently than at parties or in most homes; it related God to everyday life and showed his part in the child's happiness. A birthday chart ensured the celebration of birthdays at correct times.

A mother helped as a teacher but did not give her own child undue attention.

Notes were sent to parents the previous week to help the children remember to bring their gifts of apples. These notes also made the parents aware of what the child was doing in church school and how they might encourage similar experiences in their own families and neighborhoods.

A committee of parents worked with the teachers.

The teachers had allowed enough time for each part of the session so that they could gather the children together at the close for a kind of summary, during which they thought again of the important things of the morning.

The teachers said good-by to each child just as they had greeted each, and made sure that no one left alone.

The teachers paused briefly to make comments about the session and the next week's assignments. They parted with the idea of talking further by phone about next Sunday's plans.

Advance Planning for This Session

Since the four-year-old kindergarten was a new department in Second Church, the teachers likewise were new recruits. They got acquainted when they began working together three months prior to the October Sunday just described. The director of Christian education invited them to a meeting for general planning. In many churches the pastor, a general superintendent, or a leading teacher would do this. They decided, along with the teachers of the five-year-olds, how they would divide the big room into two departments and what equipment and materials would be needed. They looked at the enrollment cards to find the names of the children in the nursery who would be promoted to the four-year-old group. Next, they took the curriculum outline for the year and scanned it for the units of study that

they would be using in the fall, winter, spring, and summer. They read more carefully the fall units and particularly noted the purposes to be achieved with the children. The director promised to send them the fall lesson
materials as soon as they arrived in August. One further
item demanded careful planning — the first occasion the
four-year-olds would see their new room. The results
proved most worth-while. The teachers invited the children and their mothers to the room on a weekday morning before promotion Sunday. The invitations were written for different half hours so that only six or seven
children and their mothers arrived at any one time. The
children got acquainted with the teachers and played
with some of the toys. They investigated the room: they
learned about the two entrances, the hooks for wraps,
and the toilet.

In September the teachers met again and Mrs. Lynn
agreed to be the leading teacher for the first several
weeks. She acted as chairman of the meeting, and they
discussed the lesson materials they had each read at
home. They practiced the songs and selected pictures.
They chose the activities best suited to the four-year-
olds of Second Church and listed special supplies
needed. They decided on the responsibilities of each
teacher for the month. In order that they all might be
aware of the assignments of each one, they made the
following chart and put it on their wallboard:

OUR WORK FOR THIS MONTH

Unit Purpose: We Say Thank You, God
Mrs. Lynn will — be leading teacher
                 guide block building and easel paint-
                 ing
                 tell story on first and fourth Sundays

Mrs. Clark will — guide housekeeping
                     guide the color-cut-paste table
                     tell story on first and third Sundays
Mrs. Hill will — guide books and puzzles
                     interpret offering
                     tell story on second Sunday
                     teach new song on second Sunday
Mrs. Smith will — keep all records
                     get special supplies for work activities
                     get parents to help as needed

The leading teacher had other obligations besides those you observed in the session described, including an awareness of all that was happening in the room. She had made a lesson plan and was watching the clock as she used it. Because cleanup went so smoothly, she knew they had time to play the apple-seed story twice. Because there was no dawdling at the tables after work was finished, the closing conversation could be leisurely. Her lesson plan looked like this:

Purpose: To learn that we show love for others when we help them and share with them
 9:30–10:00 Informal time at interest centers
10:00–10:10 Cleanup time
10:10–10:25 Gathering together
    Review last Sunday's story by playing apple trees
    Conversation about God's plan for food and friends who help — about our gifts of apples
    Write letter to send with apples
    Sing: " Friends! Friends! Friends! "
    Donald's birthday
    Sing: " Every Morning Seems to Say "
    Read *I Peter* 5:7

Walk to picture and sit on rug
Story — Mrs. Clark
Conversation, Bible, prayer, activity — Mrs. Clark

10:25–10:35 Draw and paste pictures or go to interest centers
10:35–10:40 Conversation on rug about God's plan for food, family, friends; how we can help; how we can thank God. *I Peter 5:7.* Prayer
10:40–10:45 Get wraps
10:45 Watch for Kathy's mother to thank her
Evaluation with other teachers
Jot down carry-over for next Sunday

The very act of writing this plan impressed the day's purpose on Mrs. Lynn's mind; she knew what she hoped to accomplish and the approximate time each part of the plan would take. She was then free to use it any way she chose, even changing it all around as she worked, but rounding out the session into a complete experience. She watched for comments and questions of the children in order to make a fitting lesson plan for the next Sunday and telephoned the teachers to talk over weekly details with them. These teachers had decided to meet in the kindergarten room once a month for planning. When they met, Mrs. Lynn guided them in evaluating what they had done this first month. Then Mrs. Clark acted as chairman of the planning session, because for the approaching month she had agreed to be the leading teacher.

The parents' committee was a new venture in this kindergarten. Members of the committee helped with such simple things as searching for certain kinds of magazine pictures and getting needed materials ready for each Sunday's session. Later the committee helped by calling in the homes of absentees who lived in their neighborhoods. At the beginning of each quarter they assisted the teachers in taking the parents' material related to the curriculum into the homes. On such visits they suggested the possible re-use of each Sunday's story during the week. They suggested that songs and poems and Bible passages be used at home too. They showed the parents how they could use the materials as a family when a child had to be absent because of illness or travel.

Thus the work of this kindergarten department was done by a team of teachers who shared the more difficult parts of the work and depended upon one another. The duties of superintendent or co-ordinator, relating the four-year-old kindergarten to the entire church program, were carried by Mrs. Clark. She was the one person responsible for administrative details. But all four worked so closely that the children came to look upon each of them as " my teacher " rather than upon one of the group as " my teacher."

Chapter 8

PLANNING AS A
TEACHING TEAM

When you visited the kindergarten of Second Church
(Ch. 7), did you find it similar to the one you work in?
It is different from the average Sunday session in Amer-
ican churches of thirty years ago when a four-year-old
was told by his teacher to " find a chair in the circle, sit
still, and wait for Sunday school to begin "; after which
a superintendent led " opening exercises," and a teacher
told a story and supervised handwork at each table.

VALUES OF THE INFORMAL PROGRAM

There are valid reasons for organizing a department
as Second Church did in this informal group way. First,
a child grows best in a homelike atmosphere. Because a
preschool child is away from home for comparatively
short periods of time, it is well to organize a program in
the church that is similar to life in the home. In such a
program each child can be recognized as a person, with
his own skills and problems. He will be noticed and
loved. He will adjust to other children if he is not in a
crowd and is not forced to toe the line, but can live
with the others in a kind of larger family. He has special
needs that must be met.

Secondly, a child of this age is concerned primarily
about himself. " I " is more important than " we," but he

is ready to learn " we-ness." " I want to paint; I do not care what you want to do! " But a four-year-old is able to get along with one or two children in an activity of his own choosing. His first experiences of knowing what a group is like can best come to him in this way. Let him choose a work or play activity, and he soon becomes involved with another child. Then he thinks: *I* want to look at this book. Well, maybe *we both* could look at it. Easy and natural give-and-take occurs between the two. Then gradually he is asked to hear a story or play a game, and he finds himself in a larger group of ten to twenty children. From the time of his fourth birthday to that of his fifth, the child will travel a long way in his understanding of what " we " means. His best aid will be adults who do not coerce him but gently guide him into choosing to participate in small groups. Being together is one of the most important feelings or relationships to have. Parents and teachers of young children have the privilege of building pleasure in togetherness through informal experiences in home and kindergarten.

Thirdly, children of this age are explorers and need the joy of personally discovering life. A kindergarten department should be planned for freedom in making such discoveries as:

> What Tom will do if I hit him.
> What Jane will do if I play house with her.
> How to enjoy music.
> What is in books.
> What a teacher is — a grownup something like a parent?
> How to work with paints, blocks, and clay.

This process of discovery is actually the growing and learning referred to earlier in this book. Kindergarten rooms and sessions must be informal in order to permit and encourage such discoveries.

Fourthly, within the informal program the child develops a sense of personal responsibility for room and equipment. The kindergarten room or corner becomes his very own place in the church. He learns: " I help to clean up my room "; " I put scraps in the wastebasket "; " We care for our plants and pets."

TEACHERS PLAN AS A TEAM

Preparation for an informal kindergarten requires closer teamwork of the teachers than preparation for a formal program. In the latter, the superintendent does all of the teaching in the circle, and her assistants help by keeping the children in order when they march, listen to a story, and work at tables. In the kind of teaching we have been discussing in this book, every adult is a teacher. Each one must understand the children and be aware of the goals and weekly purposes. Each must study the lesson materials for every session. Two kinds of preparation are necessary: long-range planning and weekly planning. Both are done by individual teachers, working alone; both are done with others in department meetings. This long-range and weekly planning is like the general and the detailed planning for an extended trip. If you have ever taken a long trip, you recall that first you secured maps and information about the whole area to be visited. Then you figured out distances and where you would be each week and each day. Next you considered what you would have to pack — the kinds of clothing needed and any other things needed, such as camera, golf clubs, or books. As the time for the trip approached, you knew definitely where you were going and how you would get there, but you gave more attention to what you were packing. During the trip itself, you found that you had day-by-day choices to make, such as where to eat, what to see, how to get there. You also discovered that today's events conditioned tomorrow's; you avoided repeating the unpleasant; and you tried to duplicate the satisfying. Some of this trip planning was done alone, and some was done with your travel companions.

LONG-RANGE PLANNING ALONE

Let us consider the elements of long-range planning done alone, whether you are a parent or a teacher of four- and five-year-olds. Secure for your co-workers a supply of the chart or booklet, prepared by your denomination, outlining the kindergarten curriculum for the year. (Or if you are teaching in vacation church school, get the outline for the vacation school curriculum.) It will give the titles and purposes of the units of study as well as the Biblical backgrounds. In it you will see the whole year (or the whole vacation school) at a glance. Next, read the lesson materials for the approaching quarter. In most denominations these are composed of two items: a booklet or magazine for teachers and parents, plus a picture book or leaflets for the children. Both should be scanned or read quickly the first time for an idea of what the writer is saying. Then look more carefully to find the purpose, Biblical passages, stories, pictures, songs, activities, and supplies for each week.

Basic supplies are necessary in every session, but often extra things are needed. When both parents and teachers understand the plan for the year as well as for the quarter, they will begin to accumulate special materials for enriching the experiences of their particular children in their particular locality. For example, in a unit on God's care through his plan for growing things and for community helpers, city children may need visual helps to understand about the process of growing wheat, milking cows, raising sheep for wool. Rural children, on the other hand, might need visual help in understanding about the fireman and the street cleaner. Our churches write their curriculum materials with many kinds of communities in mind; they hope that teachers and parents will adapt the materials to the needs of their own children.

Long-Range Planning with Others

After preliminary work alone comes long-range planning with others. This is the time when all the teachers and perhaps the parents of the children get together to talk over the goals for the year and the purposes of the approaching quarter. You have done your reading alone: this meeting is the time to discuss, ask questions, and bring suggestions. As you talk, you see in your mind's eye all those delightful, mischievous children named Nancy, Marty, Ted, Jean, and Tibby. You value each one, and you are challenged to help them grow during the year toward those goals and purposes. So you begin to adapt your curriculum to fit them. Parents are most helpful in this process, for they report their own child's needs in regard to the subject at hand and see possibilities that teachers may miss.

Some groups meet once a quarter for this kind of discussion. Vacation church school teachers find it imperative to meet several times far in advance of the opening of their school. But the teaching staff of a Sunday church school feels that it needs more time together. Teachers like to meet every month or at least just before the beginning of a new unit of study, which is sometimes every six or eight weeks. They use this time not only to plan ahead but to check up on how their work is going and how it can be improved.

When the staff and parents' committee meet for such a monthly occasion, their task for planning ahead is two-fold: to make weekly teaching plans with an approximate time schedule and to determine the teaching assignments. Weekly plans include selecting and mounting pictures, planning activities, practicing songs, and considering how to build upon the experiences and responses of the children during the last session. Sometimes teachers (and parents) may try doing creative work activities such as their children will do: molding clay while music plays; painting with large brushes on large sheets of paper; using papers to cut, paste, tear, punch holes. They try to approach this work as if it were brand-new — as if they had never tried it before. The results are not judged or compared. The fun comes in doing things they may have missed when they were children — in getting the feel of it all!

Teaching assignments for the month are determined on the basis of ability and choice. A beginning teacher will not want to try the more difficult tasks until she has watched others for a few Sundays. The superintendent or co-ordinator will develop a new teacher as rapidly as she is willing to try new techniques. Each teacher or parent on the staff should have an opportunity to lead in every part at one time or another during the quarter. If a good storyteller tells the story every Sunday, no one else *becomes* a good storyteller. If a fine leading teacher holds that responsibility every Sunday, then no one else ever learns to be a leading teacher. Substitute teachers should attend these planning meetings so that they know what is taking place each month in the kindergarten. They, along with new teachers, should be trained in various techniques before they are desperately needed and called Saturday night to teach on Sunday morning. Mutual agreement on assignments means that each leader is happy in her work but is willing to exchange duties with another when family emergencies arise. A suggested chart for keeping track of such assignments is found on pages 135–137 — as one group worked this out.

An approximate time schedule is indispensable in the kindergarten. It is something like a family budget; it includes everything in proportion but frequently must yield to one or two spots of need. Some teachers plan sessions that are one hour in length, and others plan for two and three hours. The following time schedules have been used to advantage in Sunday, weekday, or vacation church schools. Time allotments fluctuate with the number of children in the group.

A One-Hour Session in Church School

Arrival and care of wraps	5 minutes
Informal work and play	15–20 minutes
Cleanup time	5–10 minutes
Group time	10–15 minutes
Work time and cleanup	10–20 minutes
Conversation or summary	2 minutes
Wraps (when needed)	5 minutes

Children who come early and are present for an hour and fifteen minutes or more gain time in the informal work and play period. This is to their advantage.

A One-Hour Session During Morning Church Service Immediately Following Church School

Toilet, washing hands	10 minutes

(Often the time between church school
and church service is used for this.)

Lunch (crackers and water), cleanup	10 minutes
Rest, putting away mats	15 minutes
Group time	20 minutes

(Correlated with the church school session in purpose, using the same Bible passage and pictures, with perhaps an additional story and song; doing some extras, such as using phonograph records, rhythm instruments, finger painting, clay, murals, outdoor work.)

Cleanup	5 minutes
Summary	5 minutes
Wraps (when needed)	5 minutes

A Two-Hour Session for Weekday or Sunday. (When used on Sunday, the second hour is usually called an extended session.)

Arrival and care of wraps	5 minutes
Informal work and play	25–30 minutes
Cleanup	5–10 minutes
Group time	20 minutes
Toilet, washing hands	10 minutes
Lunch, cleanup	10 minutes
Rest, putting away mats	15 minutes
Work time and cleanup	20–30 minutes
Summary	5 minutes
Wraps (when needed)	5 minutes

A Three-Hour Session for Weekday or Vacation School

Arrival and care of wraps	5 minutes
Informal work and play	40 minutes
Cleanup	5–10 minutes
Group time	20 minutes

Toilet, washing hands	10 minutes
Lunch, cleanup	10 minutes
Rest, putting away mats	20 minutes
Outdoors	20–30 minutes
Work time and cleanup	30 minutes
Summary	5 minutes
Wraps (when needed)	5 minutes

DEFINITION OF TERMS

Arrival and care of wraps. Includes conversation of each child with a teacher upon arrival and the process of taking off wraps and hanging them up.

Informal work and play. Includes deciding what to do, then doing it, often choosing more than one interest center in a given day.

Group time. Includes conversation, story, Bible, songs, prayer, pictures, birthdays, recognition of visitors, games, rhythms. It is so planned that the teacher hopes for moments of worship, although for some child worship might occur at the wonder table or the book corner earlier in the session.

Work time. In a short session this might include a single creative work activity or an interest center activity. In a longer session, the work can be more varied and leisurely, often more personally creative.

Cleanup. The important time during which each child gradually learns that after every job comes a time to pick up and put away — after play, after work, after lunch, after rest. The individual does his share of the work of the group.

Summary. A quiet time to talk together briefly about " our morning together " in order to highlight the meaning of the session in the children's minds in so far as words can do so. Sometimes it is done by the teacher asking one or two pertinent questions, then leading in song or prayer.

These schedules show a balance of active and inactive periods. It is as necessary for a kindergarten child to rest as to be doing something. Within each period of the day, there are shorter intervals of active and inactive times, such as when the teacher and children stand to sing after sitting still for the story, or when they take a picture walk after a group conversation.

These schedules show an approximate allotment of time; they should vary according to the age of the children, the number in the group, and the way a particular session develops. Four-year-olds need more time to put things away than fives and young sixes. Twenty children need more time for lunch or getting wraps than do seven children. A special creative activity may continue past one session and require more time for completion in two or three sessions than is ordinarily scheduled. Early in the year the children take more time for some things than later in the year. On some occasions they need a much longer time for resting — at holiday time, in extremely hot weather, and after weekends — particularly in weekday and vacation school. Parents and teachers can determine the best time schedule for a given group of children by letting the children set the pace. They must sense what is an unhurried schedule and be flexible about time allotments. Regardless of how the schedule may vary in length of periods, it remains basically the same, so that the children learn to depend on a routine with time to do this and time to do that. Within a familiar framework a child feels secure and happy, gradually learning to take the initiative in planning and working with teacher and group.

WEEKLY PLANNING WITH OTHERS

After the long-range planning is completed, it is time for the more detailed or weekly planning. When leaders live near one another, they may talk over plans between sessions, but many telephone or write notes to one another for clearing up last minute details. The leading teacher is responsible for seeing that everything is in readiness. From session to session she will watch the time schedule to see how well suited it is to the children. She will take the lead in week-by-week evaluations and will change the teaching plans made by the whole group if necessary. One group of teachers in a vacation school took a short time every day to evaluate their session and to make choices for the next day, using the following guide:

> How well did today's session go? Where were the rough spots?
>
> What must we carry over tomorrow from today? (Promising Philip he could use the easel when he first arrives; playing Cindy's game again; phoning Mrs. Gilfeather about Joy's absence.)
>
> What is our purpose tomorrow?
>
> How can we best develop it through: informal work centers? the group time? outdoor period? special activity? closing conversation?
>
> Any new supplies needed?
>
> What responsibilities will each teacher take?

This outline is usable for Sunday teaching also if the teachers can remain for a while after the children leave. It is particularly valuable to consider the first two points immediately so that each teacher can contribute pertinent observations before they are forgotten.

WEEKLY PLANNING ALONE

Every teacher plans in her own way. One developed a weekly schedule (as given below) and used it as a reminder until it became a habit.

MEMO TO ME

Through daily prayer, Bible study, and meditation, I will seek to know God's will for me and try to live it. I will ask his guidance in understanding my pupils and the ways in which they learn. I will continue to study methods of teaching so that I will improve in my relationships to the children.

I will think about the purpose of this session and be able to express it in my own words.

I will study all of the Bible passages and begin to use more than one version of the Bible. Sometimes I will incorporate the passages in my daily devotions so I can keep them in my thinking all week.

I will reread the curriculum plan for this session and note any adaptations our staff made for our children.

I will read the pupil's materials.

If I am a helping teacher, I will be ready with my specific assignment. I will have the purpose so clearly in mind that wherever I help during the entire session, I will try to achieve that purpose.

If I am the leading teacher, I will plan the session in detail:

List what must be done when I arrive early and what the first comers can do to arrange the room.

Write my time schedule so there will be plenty of time for each item.

Clear with the other teachers to be sure we all know our responsibilities.

Check the supplies to be used.

Sing the songs and practice telling the story — out loud.

Read the names of the children enrolled so that I can think of them individually and how this session may particularly help each one.

I will not feel that my teaching is finished until I have evaluated what happened. I will be frank in admitting my mistakes and humble in seeing good points.

Although it is true that each teacher plans in her own way, it is also true that some teachers do not plan thoroughly or soon enough. They find themselves searching for time and using leftover bits of energy.

EVALUATING

When you have gone on an extended trip, you return home to think of it and talk about it at every opportunity. You even discuss what you would do differently the next time. You think of the lasting values deep within that you may never be able to express to anyone else. It is the same with your teaching in the kindergarten. You are constantly striving to become a better teacher and to know whether or not the children are learning what is intended and what is planned. After the next time you teach, go home and ask yourself these questions:

Did the children seem to be at ease and happy? Did I see possible storms brewing — crying, fighting, grabbing — in time to divert them? Or if they occurred, how well did I handle them? Am I growing in my understanding of those children who are quiet and unexpressive? What must I particularly study about children this week?

What evidence do I have that learning took place today? Did I accomplish my purpose?

Did each child find something interesting to do during the informal period? Did this period show bits of learning or was it a time-filler of haphazard play and idleness?

Were my questions worded so that the children were encouraged to think? Which children need to be brought into group conversation more? How did I use the unexpected contributions?

Did I use the children's responses to the best advantage for moments of worship through wonder, song, or prayer? Was my use of the Bible meaningful or trite?

Did the timing work out as I had planned or did we have to rush through something in order to finish on time? What might I have omitted?

What did I learn from parents about the needs of any child? What did I learn from a child about his home?

What was my weakest point today? What can I do to improve?

This thoughtful type of evaluating oneself and seeking the advice of others helps a good teacher to become a better teacher. Furthermore, it makes possible a happier situation for the living and growing of young children within the Christian community.

A FORTY-HOUR WEEK?

A newcomer in the kindergarten department might cheerfully say, " It sounds as if this planning business would take eight hours a day all week! "

It does take time, but not that much. And it takes longer for the beginning worker. But like everything else one soon becomes skillful and utilizes many such minutes as those taken by dishwashing and bus riding, which require no mental activity. Such dream-gathering times might better be centered on our children!

Taking time for planning is not easy for a department group to do and first attempts may fail. But if someone with vision (whether a teacher or parent) gently persists, she will eventually have all of the leaders as traveling companions toward the goal of better experiences for children. She can be the leaven in which Jesus saw such great hope and promise in the carrying onward of his work.

Chapter 9

ORGANIZING FOR EFFECTIVE WORK

Have you ever gone to a church dinner and said to someone near you: " This is a beautiful affair! Everything is cooked perfectly and served hot. Who's in charge tonight? " You were aware that such an occasion did not just happen to be that way, but that some one person had to organize and plan with many others in order to produce a delightful whole. It could have turned out to be a jumble if the food purchasers and cooks, the table setters and decorators had not known one another's plans and timed their work. The food had to be on hand in ample time for preparation, and the tables had to be ready before decorations could be added. The women were definitely organized and functioning according to agreement.

Work in the kindergarten department demands similar organization, for there is much to be cared for behind the scenes.

WHO IS RESPONSIBLE?

Who determines the way preschool children will be grouped in a particular church, what curriculum will be used, and who will be their leaders? The governing body of the church or the Christian education committee or council plan the total organization and program. It is expected that the pastor will have an active part in this planning for young children and their parents. It is imperative that everything that happens in a church for four- and five-year-olds be co-ordinated, namely:

Sunday church school	Child care during adult
Sunday church-time care	meetings
hour	Parties and family nights
Weekday kindergarten	Vacation church school

Reasons for such co-ordination are best seen as we look at one child. What happens to Elisabeth Louise if she comes to Sunday church school, stays while her parents attend morning worship, and then comes again for weekday kindergarten, *but* is handled differently and expected to act differently during each session? For instance, for church school she may be regimented in a formal program and told just what to do; during morning service she is free to do anything because the adults in the room are only " baby sitting "; and on weekdays she is free with guidance and expected to assume responsibility for her actions and for the materials she uses. The *church* is speaking to her in three different ways and she becomes confused. Whereas by working together, the adults of all three sessions could be united in their approach to Elisabeth Louise and what they expect of her. They can and must make one strong and positive impression on each child on behalf of the *church*. They should study the purposes of Christian education and correlate the curriculum used in these three groups. The lesson materials would be developed rather fully in the church school hour, with additional purposeful activities in the church-time session, and with some repetition of story or songs in the weekday curriculum. Habits of prayer and praise will be a natural part of all the sessions. Routines for cleanup times will always be the same. Freedom to choose and act within certain bounds will be characteristic of each experience. And when a teacher of one group calls in the home, she will represent the *church*, and understanding something of the other groups Elisabeth Louise attends, will be able to answer questions about the total program for her parents. The leaders who are responsible for child care during adult meetings, church family nights, and vacation church school should be carefully instructed so that they will have the same approach with the children as the through-the-year groups.

The way in which preschool children are grouped determines in large part how well they will be able to grow and learn in the church. Small churches are to be envied, for their limited numbers make for more wholesome learning experiences. Large churches are able to keep their kindergarten departments small by having several departments or sessions. There should never be more than twenty-five children in a group, and twenty is preferable. When a church has more than that, it is best to form a four-year-old kindergarten and a five-year-old kindergarten. If there is room space, two or three departments can meet at the same hour; if not, one department can meet the first hour and another the second, using the same room. Some churches have school on Sunday afternoon also, or even on Saturday or other weekdays, in order to provide the space necessary for several departments and insure the maximum comfort and growth of each child. Because the total number of children who are this age will vary in a given church from year to year, it is possible to change the groupings in the departments. Consider the following plans:

Plan A. The four-year-olds meet together in one room.
> The five-year-olds and young sixes who have not entered first grade meet in another department.

Plan B. The four-year-olds meet together in one room.
> The five-year-olds meet in another place.
> Sixes, not yet in first grade, meet in another department.

The governing body of the church (if there is one) in co-operation with the committee on Christian education, selects the curriculum for all departments. They are the ones who are responsible for the type of materials used in the Christian nurture of the children. They are the ones who decide whether or not their denominational curriculum will be used. Whether or not this is done, they will be consistent and use one thoughtfully chosen curriculum throughout the entire school.

This official body is also the group that appoints the leaders. Members of the kindergarten staff are chosen on the basis of their earnest effort to grow in Christian living and their understanding of young children. The most mature Christians (age not being the only criterion) should be the ones who teach preschool children. Sometimes a twenty-year-old is more loving and patient than a fifty-year-old. When a child rebels, a grandmother is often more understanding than a younger mother. Most teen-agers should still be studying instead of teaching. A variety of ages and temperaments is needed, but all must be capable of Christian love and control under varying circumstances. Men as well as women become good teachers, and a " daddy " is an asset to the kindergarten. He may be the husband of one of the teachers, or he may be a man who relates well to children though he has never had any of his own. A man in the kindergarten helps to make this place of growing more like a home. And to a child whose father is dead, or whose father is not kind and loving, this man in the church home will represent fatherly concern.

THE KINDERGARTEN STAFF

The number of leaders needed in a department is one adult for every five or six children. With that number of children in the corner of a one-room church, a woman can carry on a total program of organizing and teaching, but it is wiser to have two leaders for any size group of young children in case of emergency. In a group of ten to fifteen, one person will be appointed as the superintendent, co-ordinator, or leading teacher. Both are teachers, and both have an allocated amount of organizational work to do. In a large department of fifteen to twenty-five, more workers will take part and have assigned duties. Substitute teachers should be included in all of the learning and planning meetings of the staff. Part of their training will be to work as " interns " for several Sundays so that they become familiar with the children and schedule. A parents' committee is invaluable to the kindergarten as has been pointed out many times in this book.

The competence of the staff will depend in large measure upon their regard for one another, their mutual search for knowledge, and the time they take for planning together. Chapter 8 describes how one kindergarten staff developed the process of team teaching: each carried a major share of the work every Sunday, and all were united in purpose and spirit.

THE SUPERINTENDENT

One person who is adept at details must know the kindergarten program and be able to work co-operatively with all of the others involved in it. She need not be talented in all areas of the work, for she will not *do* all of it herself. But she must be one who above all is alert and informed on what should be happening to four- and five-year-olds in the church. She must know the ongoing work of the whole department and its relationship to the whole church. This person is usually called the superintendent, and she is co-ordinator of all that is done by the staff, the parents, and the children. Being the superintendent does not necessarily mean that she is the leading teacher every Sunday. But she *is* the organizer — the starter, clarifier, nudger, spark.

The work of the kindergarten falls into five areas. The superintendent should know and discuss these areas with the other teachers in regular staff meetings. Together they will decide what is to be done by whom.

Area 1. Thorough preparation for teaching in general and for particular sessions.

Area 2. Knowledge of the children, their parents, and the homes in which they live.

Area 3. Responsibility for equipment and supplies.

Area 4. Planned teamwork with the homes.

Area 5. Responsibility for relationships to the whole church and the community.

Area 1 involves planning, learning, and working together as described rather fully in the preceding chapters. Chapter 8 points out the superintendent's responsibility to get new curriculum materials to the staff each quarter and to help them work on such materials well in advance of their use Sunday. Unless the superintendent has an intelligent grasp of the purposes of Christian education and the best ways of achieving them within the lives of children and adults, she cannot lead her staff in seeing the real meaning of the teaching program of the church. It takes continuing study to become a good leader. The job of superintendent is not the place for a person who is content to find a pattern or rut and to stay in it for many years without changing. The superintendent must be sensitive to possible change for the better and must seek outside help from leaders in and beyond her denomination.

Area 2 (*knowledge of the children*) necessitates the keeping of certain records in order that the church can express its concern for individual children and families. These deal with enrollment, attendance, birthdays, promotion, and personal growth.

Enrollment records should include: the name of the child, address, phone, birth date, parents' names and their church affiliation, names of others in the household. In a large church or one of changing families, it is well to have an interview between parent and superintendent when a child is enrolled. This can begin for the whole department at promotion if word is sent to the parents of the incoming children that the superintendent will be in the kindergarten room on a certain day for fifteen-minute visits with each child and parent. Definite appointment times are made by a parent. During this informal conversation, the child gets acquainted with both his new teacher and his new room. (Or if he has been there before, he enjoys it all to himself!) The superintendent has arranged the room as it is on Sundays (or on weekdays if it is a weekday or vacation church school the child is entering) by putting the interest centers in order and placing clay, paints, crayons, scissors, and paste on a table for use. While the child is occupied in one part of the room, the parent and teacher may be able to talk freely about him and his interests in another part. The following questionnaire is a guide for note-taking. Such a sheet for each child will begin the continuing personal record of his church experiences, which is referred to later. The letter is a copy of one used by a team of teachers who wanted to know their children before vacation school began. Inasmuch as registration was requested in advance, they were able to get the names of the children and write to the parents. They used the first day for personal interviews instead of for a session of the whole group.

Many Sunday church schools now require for all ages an annual re-enrollment and interview or orientation session with parents. It is obvious that changing family situations and the child's own development make this wise.

Getting Acquainted with a Child

This information will aid the teachers to help each child have satisfactory experiences in the kindergarten.

Name of child _____

Date of birth _____

Parents' names _____

Address _____ Phone _____

Favorite play materials _____
_____

Favorite occupations _____

Pets _____

What opportunities does he have to be with children his own age?
_____

Special problems: Fears _____ Food _____.
Health _____ Susceptibility to colds _____
Special Experiences: Hospital _____ Travel _____
Any others _____

Adults in home, besides parents (relationship as well as name)

_____

Other children in family: Names, ages

_____

_____

Church membership, father _____
Church membership, mother _____

Dear Mr. and Mrs. _____

We are happy to have your child enrolled in the vacation church school of the First Presbyterian Church, June 17–27. Mrs. _____, the assistant teacher, and I will be at the church Monday morning and afternoon, June 16, for a brief conversation with the children and their mothers or fathers. We are eager to get acquainted before the school opens. Mrs. _____ will make appointments at fifteen-minute intervals, so will you please phone her for the time you prefer? (Main 6121.)

The teaching purpose in vacation school this summer is as follows: to welcome children into the church as Jesus welcomed children and to guide them in learning what children and adults do in the church.

It is increasingly true that Christian parents are giving considerable thought to the privilege and responsibility of Christian nurture. Would you be interested in discussing with other parents and teachers how we can lay a sound foundation for Christian faith and life, which will deepen as the children mature? It may be that the fathers and mothers of nursery and kindergarten children will want to have such an evening together early in the second week of the school.

If you have any suggestions regarding your child, do feel free to make them, so that we teachers can plan with you for his well-being and happiness during vacation school days.

Cordially yours,

Kindergarten Superintendent

No great stress is placed on perfect attendance in the kindergarten because children of this age are dependent upon adults and cannot control their attendance. It is more important for teachers to watch the records to see who is absent and check up with the family of the absentee. Sniffles or trips often keep a child away, but prolonged illness or apathy of the parents may be the cause. For both of these latter reasons the church should express its concern.

Birthdays are special days in families; they are a time when the friendship of church school teachers is appreciated. It means much for a child (and his parents) to receive a birthday card through the mail on his day. Some teachers make a birthday calendar and post it on the teachers' or parents' bulletin board at the church. Under each month they list the date and child's name. This serves as a weekly reminder for the person who sends the cards and for the leading teacher who recognizes the child on his birthday Sunday. The way of doing so that is now generally accepted is indicated on page 129.

The best time for promotion is thought by many to be early fall. When teachers look at promotion as both coming in and going out, they realize that there is a double approach to the day. The children coming in from the nursery will be going through a new and strange experience; their teachers and parents must prepare them in advance. The kindergarten staff can assist by planning for personal visits to the room as suggested earlier. Then it is possible to avoid upsetting experiences such as caused these tearful comments by two four-year-olds, " My mommy doesn't know where I am " and " My coat is in the other room." Some churches plan this moving up for nursery children as individuals, or make the change for small groups at appropriate intervals.

The children who are going out of the kindergarten need similar help to be ready for promotion. Let them visit the primary department for part of a session near promotion time. Invite the primary superintendent to visit them in the kindergarten. Plan for her to use some of the well-loved kindergarten songs, pictures, and books for two or three Sundays in the primary department during the adjustment time.

Promotion in the preschool departments should be based on the age required in your community for entrance into first grade. For example, if your schools require a child to be six years old by December 1 in order to enter first grade in the fall, then the children who are promoted into the primary department should be that age and entering first grade. You can organize your five-year-old kindergarten for those children who will be five before December 1; they will enter first grade and the primary department together the next year. The four-year-old department can be for children who will be four by December 1, and the nursery can enroll children in the fall who will be three before December 1. If the grading in the church school is kept in line with the public school, it is easier for both children and parents.

Records of personal growth should be kept for each child. If the teacher is to be an understanding friend to a child, it is essential that she know whether or not there are brothers and sisters, whether there are two parents or only one, whether there are grandparents living in the home. Long illnesses of family members make an imprint on the child and often cause different behavior, as do travel, business changes, and moving. Church membership and attendance (or lack of it) influences what the teacher may wish to discuss when she calls in the home. Comments of the child in the session, activities he chooses or doesn't choose, may be jotted down on his record card. Over a period of time they make a picture of the child and help the teacher to understand him and to provide learning situations that seem to meet his needs. It is wise to keep these cards confidential. The information should be available only to those who are working for the growth of the child and who will not use it in idle conversation.

Personal records begin for some children when the kindergarten staff calls in new homes and on unchurched families in the community who have four- and five-year-olds. Teachers do this in the spirit of wanting others to be a part of the fellowship of the church, of wanting young and old to know and love God through Jesus Christ.

Area 3 (*responsibility for equipment*) deals with the selection and care of equipment and supplies. Although the governing body of the church is initially responsible for the kindergarten room, the teachers who work in it share this obligation. They must see that furnishings are kept clean and in good repair. The old phrase " cleanliness is next to godliness " could well be remembered by church teachers. Too frequently no one feels responsible for washing toys and doll clothes, mending a rip in the rug, painting the furniture, washing the woodwork. Things should be immaculate for the children of the church.

Next to cleanliness is neatness, which applies particularly to another item, namely, the teachers' cupboard. Is it a veritable no man's land in your department? Do all use it and none keep it in order? Have things accumu-

lated through many years and does no one discard useless articles? The superintendent with her teachers
should organize the way they will keep supplies, then
label the shelves so all will remember and use the plan.
There are many household items that can be used in the
church school. A metal carrier for water glasses is handy
for carrying jars of paint from cupboard to table, floor,
or easel. Muffin tins are useful for keeping odd items in
order — thumbtacks, paper clips, gummed labels, stick-
ers, rubber bands, pins. Shelves an inch or two apart
and the size of curriculum pictures can be built into a
deep cupboard for a picture file. Such shelves should be
labeled and pictures filed (after current use is over) by
subjects, such as Christmas, Easter, Jesus at work, God's
world, community helpers, the church, friends, and family life. Neatness in the cupboard makes for enjoyment
and efficiency in each Sunday's work. It is understood
that teachers in the weekday and vacation school kindergarten will also co-operate in this care of materials. The superintendent is accountable for keeping an
adequate supply of materials on hand.

Area 4 (*planned teamwork with homes*) rightly includes a parents' committee. A good kindergarten program for the children includes their parents, and this is
evident in the small church where everyone knows everyone else. In larger areas, many weekday nurseries
and kindergartens will not enroll a child unless the parents agree to be part of the program; an interview is
held before the child is enrolled; and the parents are requested to attend certain meetings and serve in the
school during the year. Churches usually have not made
such stipulations except in some weekday church kindergartens. Many are beginning to require the inter-

view because they see its inestimable worth in making a direct and immediate bond between home and church. Parent and teacher are at once thrown into a friendly relationship based on their interest in a particular child. The parent has an opportunity to express his concerns for the child: " This is his first school experience. I do not know how he will behave," or " She is afraid to leave me because I was in the hospital for a month this summer, so may I attend with her until she feels happy about staying alone? " At the same time, the interview gives the teacher an opportunity to discuss the purpose of the kindergarten and how this purpose can be accomplished in the life of the child by home and church working in partnership.

After this initial acquaintance, it is natural for the superintendent to invite the parents to visit on a certain Sunday. She asks the person responsible for home contacts to phone one or two sets of parents a week, depending on the size of the room and whether it can accommodate two or four visitors at a given time. When parents observe a regular session, they can see and later share their child's interest in friends and in certain activities. A brief guidance sheet or a talk with the leading teacher before the session begins will help in this procedure.

Some superintendents believe that further contacts with the parents are best secured through a parents' committee of two or three couples or key parents. Such superintendents work with these chosen adults to plan ways of meeting the needs of parents. The parents should, of course, take the lead in setting up and carrying out any project. The enthusiasm of these young couples is caught by others and reacts upon indifferent parents in a positive way. Friendships begin and spiritual concerns are awakened; the fellowship of kindred minds takes form for them in the body of the church. Such a process may begin through one of the following activities planned by the parents' committee or key parents in co-operation with the superintendent and teachers, the pastor or director. Several of them can be planned by more than one church, interdenominationally (especially Nos. 2, 4, 5, 6). Invite all of the children's parents (sometimes a guardian or grandparent is acting the role of a parent) to the kindergarten room on a weekday evening. At such a time you may:

1. Plan a friendly time so all will get acquainted if they do not already know one another. Then describe in detail what happens in this room on Sunday morning (or on a weekday if the vacation or weekday school is sponsoring this event) and why. Sing the songs being used that month; interpret the simple Bible verses as basic learning for larger concepts later in life; show how the children are taught to pray; look at some of the teaching pictures and discover what the children find in them. Recall incidents of actual learning that have taken place and report them without disclosing the names of the children involved. Show paintings, drawings, clay and block work — not by sorting out the " best " by your standards but by exhibiting some one thing of every child's as worth-while in the growing process. Encourage questions throughout.

2. Listen for the questions that parents ask personally and see if they may not need to talk together about how children grow. A film such as *The Frustrating Fours and Fascinating Fives* (see page 192) reveals that all children grow through the same phases. It is heartening to parents to know that others have the same joys and

problems, and it induces them to share their own experiences and questions. All this might lead to a series of discussions.

3. If your meeting is at the beginning of the year or of a new quarter, survey the curriculum and its purposes for the coming months. Plans for such a meeting are given on page 143 under "Long-Range Planning with Others." Parents are usually curious about what happens in the kindergarten and do not get satisfying answers when they question their children. Such a preview can create interest in the wider subject of the purposes of Christian education and the ways children learn. If an interest is picked up immediately, it can lead to further discussions, conversations, and reading.

4. Discover whether or not your parents are being asked difficult questions by their children, such as: Where is God? Who made him? What is dying like? Do puppies go to heaven? What is Easter? Perhaps they would like help in answering such questions. Secure a strong resource person to help them think through the answers and to speak to them on how a child's faith grows. Good books (see pages 191–192) should be at hand to lend to the parents. Such discussions sometimes grow into a regular class for young couples who want to study their own faith and grow in comprehension of it.

5. Arrange a workshop during which parents can learn the values of various art media used with children. Place a different kind of work on each table and let the parents move from one to another, so that only a few are at each table at one time. Let them try clay, finger painting, brush painting, cutting gay papers, collage, a mural. They might like to build with the educational

blocks and try the rhythm instruments. Simple directions are given by a teacher or parent at each table. Encourage the adult who is slow to take part. Be sure that everyone knows this is an experimental fun time and finished products are not important. The purpose is to do, to feel, to enjoy. Then have a qualified person talk on the values of such activities for young children. Tell where they may secure art materials and borrow books (see pages 191–192) for further reading.

6. Try a parent-child-teacher dessert party in the early evening immediately after dinners at home. A few simple games, songs, and stories should complete the party in an hour. This more unusual kind of affair helps some parents to discover how to play and have fun with children of this age.

There are many other ways for parents and teachers to keep close together in the nurture of their children. You may want to try the following:

Arouse interest in planning together for enriching Christian family life and learning more about the spiritual guidance of the children there.

Stimulate parents to use the church curriculum at home.

Have a bulletin board for parents just outside the kindergarten door and keep it freshly stocked with pertinent items related to Christian growth, such as covers from books added to the church library.

Keep a small library of books in circulation for the use of parents.

Call in the homes of unchurched families.

Motivate couples to plan imaginative types of family worship in their homes.

Help new families to become involved in the total life of the church.

See that parents know of individuals (including the minister) and agencies available to them when counseling is needed.

Give comfort and guidance to families broken by divorce or death or interrupted by long illnesses.

Area 5 (*responsibility for relationships to the church as a whole and the community*) involves the relationship of the kindergarten staff to the rest of the church school through its superintendent, who attends meetings of all the departmental superintendents when *general* plans are necessary. These may be concerned with such special parts of your program as promotion, Every Member Canvass, family nights, Christmas, vacation school. The superintendent carries to this group the desire of the kindergarten staff to protect their children from experiences not suited to their age. She works through this body to co-ordinate weekday activities that affect four- and five-year-olds and their parents, such as child care during the women's organization meeting. She becomes familiar with any problems the sexton may have in relation to the kindergarten room or the yard. She learns what amount of money is available for regular and seasonal supplies for the kindergarten. She also represents the best interests of four- and five-year-olds when community affairs affecting children are planned. The kindergarten staff can speak on behalf of supervised playground space and early evening hours for neighborhood functions. They can take a stand, if they care to, against Sunday parades that bring Santa Claus to town in the fall and Mr. Easter Bunny in the spring. An alert superintendent and teachers are influential in many ways that have to do with young children.

In summary, the work of organizing the kindergarten department is one that involves a vast number of details. But once they are all seen in proportion and relationship, each member of the staff can be encouraged to do his or her share. It is expected that teachers understand the organizational pattern and terminology within their own denomination. A smooth departmental organization, however, requires the vigilance of a superintendent who sees that all necessary planning and doing happens at the proper times, with friendly co-operation, and with personal satisfaction and growth on the part of each and every staff member.

Chapter 10

THE ADULTS CHILDREN NEED

A four-year-old stood crying in the crowded hall just before time for morning church service. Several adults tried to pacify her. Presently her kindergarten teacher came by and said: "Hello, Jane! I'll help you find Daddy!" The child stopped crying as she walked hand in hand with her teacher. When they found Daddy, the child spoke first, saying: "Look, Daddy! See who I found!" and her face radiated happiness and content. There was no further trace of unhappiness in being lost; there was only complete joy in finding a friend who cared. Her sense of security was regained even before she found her parent.

Such a relationship between teacher and child is important. It makes the church a place where there is understanding and love and helpfulness among people. This kind of relationship should exist with other adults in the church too — such as the church school secretary and the superintendent, the minister, the organist, the sexton. Contacts with other members of the church family are equally important. It is of great value to the child to be recognized as a person by adults — through a smile, a greeting by name, a question about his activities. Because adults constantly reflect the quality of

their thinking and living, children should have the privilege of associating with consecrated Christians who
daily seek to do God's will. All experiences with people
in the church should reflect Christian love and concern
so that the child begins to feel and know certain things
about church. To him the church may be a building at
first, but soon it must become people who do and say
helpful things in a warm and friendly way. " How did
you get so nice? " asked a little girl as she patted the
teacher. So it is that the church is a good place to be, a
loving family, a fellowship of the concerned; for, " we
love, because he first loved us."

ADULTS WHO INCLUDE CHILDREN

Anne was only eight years old, but the following incident will show that her short life had already been
deeply and positively influenced by church-minded
adults. One winter Anne, her brother, their parents and
grandparents went to their church each Sunday evening
for a series of family nights. The evenings began with a
potluck supper, followed by family devotions around
the tables, then mission study classes for each age group.
The committee in charge decided that on the last night
all the classes would meet together to summarize what
they had learned. They would have a panel with repre-
sentatives from each class. So one of the committee telephoned Anne and asked if she would represent the primary department on the panel. She said she would have
to think it over. After a half hour alone in her room, she
went to her mother and said: " I've decided to do it. I
got more yeses than noes." Anne told her mother that
many reasons for doing and for not doing what was
asked had come to her mind, so she wrote them on paper. She did not want to do it because she would be

"scared" and because she did not "know enough" about migrants. "But," she went on, "this is the first time my church has asked me to do anything. And I've noticed that when the church asks you and Daddy to do something, you usually do it. So I'm going to do it."

For only eight short years Anne had lived with parents who took part in the work and worship of the church, and their pattern of life had made a deep impression on her. Anne had been regular in attending church school since she was three years old. Now she too wanted to be a helping part of her church — an idea that had been fostered in the nursery and kindergarten departments as well as at home. Now she felt a new association with older boys and girls, with young people and with adults. The meaning of "the church" was enlarging for Anne.

ADULTS WHO UNDERSTAND CHILDREN

Certain adults seem to help children more than others. Who are they? What are they like? What do they do? These adults — whether parent, teacher, or friend — are undoubtedly fond of children and enjoy having them around. But usually their fondness is more than a natural liking. It is threefold, including an understanding (in general) of children and their needs; a respect for the individual child and his right to grow in his own way; a willingness to put aside personal desires for the welfare of the child for whom they are responsible to God.

In attempting to understand children and their needs we are apt to think first of food, clothing, and shelter as minimum necessities. We say that each newborn child has the "right" to expect these necessities. We also recognize the fact that it is necessary to know how a child is growing; how he changes from one stage to another; what kind of guidance he must have from adults for good changes; what kinds of toys and work materials are helpful as he learns to live. But it is vital that certain basic emotional needs are fully met. The child must have plenty of the following:

Love. He needs
> — to be loved and accepted without reserve, especially when he does and says the wrong things!

Security. He needs
> — to belong to a group and to feel accepted in it; first in the family, then neighborhood, church, school.
> — to feel the meaning of togetherness in " we " and " our." Along with the importance of " I " and " me " comes the need for knowing and liking " we " and " us."

Accomplishment. He needs
> — to accomplish things and be appreciated for carrying them through. He must not be ignored, overpowered, or treated as a toy or puppet, but as a worth-while person.

Pleasure through his senses. He needs
> — to have experiences of beauty and joy in feeling things, in smelling, tasting, hearing, and seeing.

These are basic emotional needs of every human being and are applicable to all ages. All people need a continuance of love, security, accomplishment, and pleasure through the senses during their entire lives. Parents and teachers who are aware of these emotional needs will strive to fulfill them for each child. Thus the child grows into a wholeness or completeness at every stage of life that makes for security and satisfaction.

Secondly, adults must have a respect for the individual child and his right to grow in his own way. A common tendency among parents and teachers is to tell a child too often what to do and how, when, and where to do it — " Do what Mother wants," " Do what Daddy asks," " Do what teacher says." Adults who constantly make these demands use a child as a puppet who does what the manipulator causes him to do. They expect one kind of behavior from all children; and their dominance often secures their version of ideal behavior from the children, at least for a while. Meantime, the children become dependent for direction and do not think for themselves.

It is more difficult but much more realistic to look at each child as he is — a new creation of God, with undreamed-of potential gifts. It is the duty and privilege of adults to live with each child in such a way that his unique gifts will unfold and develop to the full. They should provide him with freedom to make choices in an environment where a variety of resources can be explored. They should give him time to discover and to learn at his own speed. Because God made him in a certain way, he needs to grow and should have the right to grow in that way. There are slow learners and fast learners; there are buoyant temperaments and phlegmatic temperaments; there are artistic natures and mechanical natures. A father of nine children called them his " samples " because " each is different from the other."

Children need adults who can accept them as they are and help each to become what God intends.

The third way in which certain adults help children is by their willingness to put aside personal desires for the welfare of the child for whom they are responsible to God. Christian parents recognize that their child is a trust from God. It is often essential for them to give up personal pleasure so that they can remain with their child and be sure he is feeling secure and wanted and loved. Correspondingly, teachers in the church recognize that as church members they too have responsibility for the nurture of children. They often give up leisure-time diversions in order to spend hours of work in planning and preparing for meaningful experiences for their kindergarten children. But neither parent nor teacher regrets such self-denial, for to them the child's welfare comes first. And they will seek for occasions that help them grow in understanding and skill, such as parent-teacher meetings, family camps, leadership training weekends and schools.

Adults Who Plan Thoughtfully for Children

Think for a few minutes about your favorite child — a neighbor, a niece or a nephew, a pupil, a son or daughter, as grandchild. If you could give one important gift during a lifetime to him or to her, what would it be? What, beyond all else, do you hope this child will have, know, or become? You look down the years at the mass of experiences he will face. Perhaps you think:

If only he can have true love of family and friends . . .

If only I could protect him from suffering. No, it is a necessary part of his life . . .

I hope that he will know the satisfaction of doing hard work well.

I hope that he will be able to rise above disappointments and to be humble in successes.

I hope that he will not be self-centered, but will seek to help others.

So it would go, the list getting longer and longer until you stop to ask, "What will encompass all this?"

Maturing Christian adults know from experience that their personal relationship to God in Christ is the central force in their lives. Through it they have found God's love to be a creative power in all relationships. The church of Christ has become a source of strength as well as a channel for service. They have learned to turn to the Bible for knowledge of God and his will. These adults covet for their children the beginning of such a relationship to God so they too may respond to his call — when it comes — as committed disciples.

In our mobile society many families attend whatever church is nearest to their homes. Often it is not the same denomination in which the parents were reared. These adults become confused about their faith; or they may consider it their duty to accept without question what their new church teaches. But in all evangelical churches of the Reformed tradition, there is a basic oneness in faith. Adults in any of them can continue to study so that their personal beliefs are clarified and deepened. In order to work effectively with children, parents and teachers must know their faith and how their chosen denomination puts that faith into action.

The plans that such churches have for training their children are most clearly expressed in the curriculum or lesson materials they publish. Editors and writers are persons who give full time (or a great deal of time) to the study of Christian nurture. Together with many teachers and parents they build a curriculum for their denomination that will guide a child in such a way that he is capable of attaining deeper comprehensions in each new stage of development. The curriculum of a denomination is published only after many people have outlined, written, read, and criticized it. Periodically — in some instances continually — it is re-evaluated to make sure that theological and educational standards are maintained, that Biblical interpretations are consistent with the denomination's faith, and that the outreach program of that church is interpreted correctly. Teachers who use the curriculum of their denomination are often consulted by the editors about their use of it in order to contribute to its improvement.

Curriculum materials published by nondenominational houses are not to be confused with or used interchangeably with denominational materials. They are written and edited under the direction of a commercial publishing house, not a church, and therefore may teach doctrine inconsistent with the faith of one's own denomination. Local churches have no control of what is written in such lesson materials; whereas within their denominational curriculums, they may criticize and make suggestions to the representative body responsible for setting policy for their curriculum materials.

As a teacher or parent you will be interested in securing descriptive material from your own denominational headquarters outlining its total curriculum. How does your church plan to train its growing members? Of course, you will want to study particularly its plan for kindergarten children and how it fits into the whole. Note the statements of purpose, the units of work, and

how these and the particular sessions are developed to
move toward some part of the general purpose. When
you next prepare to teach, you will see that the curriculum planned for four- and five-year-olds is a guide for
knowing what part of the over-all purpose they are
probably ready to learn. How you use it with individual
children will depend on how well you understand each
child's needs.

Other adults in the church besides parents and teachers affect the lives of children. Adult committees that
plan family nights, the keeping of Christmas and Easter,
weekday kindergartens, vacation church schools, and
church-time care groups must have an understanding
viewpoint toward the preschool child. If adults do not
sense the importance of these early years, they will plan
occasions that are detrimental to children, occasions
that do not truly represent God's church to this age
child. For instance, some adult committees permit children of all ages to have a haphazard playtime during
the morning church service. It is better to use this time
for small groups of about the same age, with good leaders who will make a plan correlated with the church
school curriculum. Some adults do not hesitate to allow
four- and five-year-olds to meet in a room with sixty or
more children. For good personal growth, kindergarten
children should be in a room with twenty or less. This
is possible in most churches in a number of ways: by re-
assigning space, by planning thoughtfully for expansion,
by having more than one church school session — even
by encouraging the establishment of a new church!

Some adults plan for the entire school to meet together for a program on Christmas and Easter Sundays;
but the meaning of these major days can usually be better interpreted within the preschool group. Often adults

plan giving projects for the church school and expect nursery and kindergarten children to give money too. Money has little if any meaning to these children and cannot help them at this stage to learn the spirit of sharing. Giving projects should be adapted to these departments so that giving can be tangible or made clear to the children by planned experiences or good family co-operation. Some adult committees ask persons who are immature to teach " the little ones " or " the babies." They do not realize that a high degree of maturity and skill is essential for teaching preschool children. They do not offer training to new teachers, nor do they supervise and guide them after they have accepted a teaching responsibility. How important are adult committees to the welfare of children!

It is true that many things happen in churches that result in negative learning unworthy of the name of the church. It is also true that the adults who are responsible for such situations are often unaware of the harm they do. Therefore, it behooves any one person who sees and understands the needs of preschool children to speak on their behalf. Such a person can get books by recognized authors in this field for adult committee members to read. With the co-operation of the pastor or superintendent, a preschool psychologist or educator might be secured (possibly from the church's own membership) to study the program for the young child and speak to the responsible adults about the impressions being made on their children in that program.

ADULTS WHO ENDEAVOR TO GROW IN CHRISTIAN FAITH AND WITNESS

We have previously said that a young child learns first from what we are as parent or teacher, without hearing us say a word. This indicates that if we adults hope to teach Christianity, we can do so only by being mindful of our own Christian living. No Christian feels that he has attained perfection, so he keeps striving with God's help to order his motives, feelings, actions, and words in the hope that he will faithfully reflect his beliefs. We are supported on all sides in our striving by several sources from which we may receive help.

The first is the nurture and fellowship of the church. As members of the church we are associating with others who have heard God speak and have answered his call. We discover that we are teacher and pupil at one and the same time in this community of believers, for as we worship and study and work, we learn from one another. We are teachers one of another; we are pupils one of another; we are truly responsible for one another.

This fellowship we call the church has been called by other names that attempt to describe its nature: the community of believers, a fellowship of the concerned, a fellowship of sinners, not merely the fellowship of the saved but the adventurous fellowship of the saving. Whatever terms we accept as our idea of the church, when we become teachers within it, our actions and words must be consistent with our belief. Can we love the dirty tousle-haired boy every bit as much as Deacon Jones's immaculate son? Can we be glad that Betsy likes another teacher better? Do we give ample time to planning with our team of teachers? Are we free to make suggestions to them and ready to accept criticism from them? Knowing that knowledge and attitudes are important, do we resist condemning a co-worker whose attainments in either or both are obviously limited for an adult Christian? Do we find occasions for studying and discussing our faith so that we are prepared to answer aright the questions children ask? It is in such relationships that we can become more nearly what God intends us to be.

A second source of strength is prayer. We need not feel alone in the teaching task; God can use us in spite of our limitations if we combine hard work with prayer. No problem is too small to take to him, no joy too great. We know that we can do "far more abundantly than all that we ask or think" if we conscientiously bend ourselves to his will. In prayerful living we find he is indeed the unseen companion who is "closer than breathing." Such prayer must be continuing — for a better understanding of self, for a clear perception of God's will, for the true sharing of his concern for the children we teach.

Closely linked to prayer is a third source of help for growth in Christian stature — Bible study. There are many plans for Bible study, but we must each find those which help us most: studying one book at a time, the life of one person, the rise and fall of a nation, one incident, or one idea, such as grace, forgiveness, obedience, the Holy Spirit.

Sometimes a teacher of young children reads only those portions of the Bible that are used with the children. This limits her own growth. Most of the denominational curriculum or lesson materials supply guidance for adult Bible study, which is related to the material for the children. Once read, such passages can be thought over during daily work in order to be fully absorbed and seen in relation to today's world as well as to next Sunday's session. If we let God speak to our reading, he will open new understanding; the same Bible passage read at ages ten, twenty, and forty becomes new and exciting with the added years of maturity. But this takes personal discipline in individual study as well as in the group Bible study planned by many churches for their adult members.

Have you ever read one of the Gospels with the purpose of discovering how Jesus taught? What was important to him as a teacher? Did he seek first of all to convey information from the sacred books? What was his attitude toward people? How did he go about meeting the need of each individual? When we study the teaching procedures of Jesus, we find much that can help us as teachers of children.

A fourth source comes through the many learning opportunities that help adults grow in teaching skills — the use of storytelling, music, creative work activities, pictures, and other methods and materials. Reference books are listed in denominational curriculums and at the back of this volume; they can be found in public and church libraries. Often there is a leadership training class in an individual church or in an interdenominational community leadership school. There are those kindergarten teachers who have been at the job conscientiously for a long time, not only in weekday and Sunday church schools but also in the public schools. Help could be gained from such people by visiting to watch them teach children, or even by an interview with them about kindergarten teaching. An able teacher who finds joy in her work is always willing to help one who is beginning. There are also summer laboratory schools where adults can observe a teacher who excels in work with children and at the same time can take a course in kindergarten work. The learning gained in these ways is as helpful to parents as it is to teachers.

Since adults are of such great importance to the Christian nurture of young children — adults who are loving and helpful, patient and understanding — it is essential that a church use wisdom and great care in choosing those who are to deal with children. It is the quality of such persons that matters. Teachers should be emotionally stable and spiritually mature. Of course, parents cannot be " chosen," but the church should take seriously the matter of strengthening and enriching the homes of its children. Often young parents are so involved in earning a living and caring for a family that they are not fully aware of what the church fellowship can mean to them and to their children. So the pastor or director of Christian education, or the superintendent and the whole kindergarten staff, should take time to think together about how to make the church vital to such parents. Parents sometimes need help without fully realizing or expressing their hunger.

As the Christian growth of parents and teachers continues and their understanding and commitment deepens, this will be evident to young children in many ways, both apparent and intangible. For in such lives and homes, there will be a trust and faith that meets small irritations and large disasters with serenity; a sure foundation for choices and decisions; a willingness to forgive and seek forgiveness. In time, the child will begin to understand that these grownups he loves turn to God for the same kind of guidance he receives from them. For some children this comes about through everyday experiences, such as family worship, grace at meals, observing Father or Mother read the Bible or pray alone. A woman who knew none of these as a child, having grown up in a home where God was not honored, began to know him through a church school teacher when she was seven. So it was that her first idea of God was that of a wonderful friend. Another woman experienced parental trust in God through a crisis. She recalls that when she was five, the family barn burned down when struck by lightning in a storm. There was no cursing of the elements or of God. She recalls the calmness with which her father explained to her older brother that green hay attracts electricity, and even though he had left open the doors of the barn for ventilation, this was probably the reason that lightning had struck. "Everything will be all right," the father reassured, "we will just have to build another barn."

All adult members of the church have responsibility for the children whether or not they are parents, teachers, or members of committees. In some churches at the time of Baptism or dedication, a child is commended to the care of the entire membership. Young and old grow together in the church. Someone has said, "You can't be human alone." It is equally true that we cannot be Christians alone. We need one another; in fact, we must depend upon one another for growing in the Christian life. Four- and five-year-olds especially need to be persons in the church — persons recognized and wanted by adults, helped and understood by adults, nurtured in Christian love at all times by the adults of the church.

Jesus said: " I am the true vine, and my Father is the vinedresser. Every branch of mine that bears no fruit, he takes away, and every branch that does bear fruit he prunes, that it may bear more fruit."

" Abide in me, and I in you. As the branch cannot bear fruit by itself, unless it abides in the vine, neither can you, unless you abide in me. I am the vine, you are the branches. He who abides in me, and I in him, he it is that bears much fruit, for apart from me you can do nothing."

" By this my Father is glorified, that you bear much fruit, and so prove to be my disciples. As the Father has loved me, so have I loved you; abide in my love."

" These things I have spoken to you, that my joy may be in you, and that your joy may be full."

" You did not choose me, but I chose you and appointed you that you should go and bear fruit and that your fruit should abide."

— John 15:1–2, 4–5, 8–9, 11, 16

For Further Thinking

Chapter 1

1. Observe a four-year-old. How does he compare with an older five-year-old in physical abilities? in social relationships?
2. Look in your records for the names of two children who are the same age in years and months. Watch them for several weeks. How are they alike? how different?
3. Which two or three children in your kindergarten do you tend to completely overlook? Why? Try to learn something about their interests and families.
4. Because five-year-olds usually have good control of arms and legs and only fair control of hands and feet, how do these physical characteristics affect what you plan for them to do in church school?

Chapter 2

1. Think of the last time you taught four- and five-year-olds. What happened in that session that appealed to each of the senses — feeling, seeing, tasting, smelling, hearing?
2. Explain to a grandmother what is meant by " The story and Bible verse are not necessarily ' the lesson.' "
3. How can you keep alive that vital spark in every child known as curiosity? Are you dulling it with too many teacher-directed activities and teacher rules?

Chapters 3, 4, 5

1. How can freedom to do his own planning and work at this age help a child in his self-esteem? How can freedom to work as he wants affect his attitude toward work all of his life?
2. Are you as an adult afraid to draw? paint? use clay? Can you recall why? Try one of these activities just for the pleasure of letting go and doing it.
3. Give reasons for including dolls, blocks, and other toys in the church kindergarten. What are the disadvantages of using them when teachers are not aware of the real purposes in doing so?
4. Does your kindergarten schedule include rest? What kind is most useful in a one-hour session?

Chapter 6

1. After reading this chapter, draw a plan of your kindergarten room and ask: How does the arrangement of furniture indicate distinct

centers of interest? Does it provide adequately for each? Can the furniture be easily moved for certain group activities?
2. What makes a room a good place for Christian nurture? What can the teacher's personality add to this?

Chapter 7

1. What routines can be established in the kindergarten in regard to wraps? putting away work and play materials? the offering? ventilation?
2. Think of yourself as a visitor in your room last Sunday. Describe and evaluate the session.

Chapter 8

1. Describe how the teachers in your kindergarten plan their work together. Can this procedure be improved? How?
2. How does your staff evaluate its work? How do you share with one another your findings from reading and study?
3. As an individual teacher, how do you go about planning for each session? In what way could you do this better?

Chapter 9

1. If you could plan for the very best growth of the preschool children in your church, what in particular would you do for the four-year-olds? the six-year-olds who are not yet in the first grade?
2. What is the value of having men teach four- and five-year-olds? What characteristics would you look for in seeking such a man?
3. What is the function of a superintendent? of a leading teacher?
4. Why is it important for parents to be involved in church plans for their children? What are you doing about this in your church?

Chapter 10

1. Try to recall an experience in your own childhood with an adult in your church. Why was it pleasant? unpleasant? How did you feel toward the church because of that person?
2. Does your church use the curriculum materials published by your denomination? If not, why? Who determines what is used — minister, teachers, committee on Christian education?
3. What books have you read in the past year that dealt with teaching kindergarten children? with the Christian faith? Turn to " Selected Readings " (pages 191–192) for suggested titles.

4. Discover dates for the leadership training schools of your denomination and of the National Council of Churches. Talk over the possibility of attending such with other teachers from your church.

Selected Readings

Unless otherwise indicated, the books and materials listed here can be ordered through your denominational book stores. Availability and prices change constantly, so the latter are not included. Consult your Christian education headquarters for other recommended books.

1. *To discover what children are like:*
   Almy, Millie, *Child Development*
   Jenkins, Gladys G., and others, *These Are Your Children*
   Strang, Ruth, *A Study of Young Children*
   Your Child from One to Six, Superintendent of Documents, Government Printing Office, Washington 25, D.C.
2. *To understand why children behave as they do and how an adult responds:*
   Havighurst, Robert J., *Developmental Tasks and Education*
   Hymes, James L., Jr., *Understanding Your Child*
   ———*A Child Development Point of View*
   ———*Behavior and Misbehavior*
3. *To become informed on kindergarten procedures and standards in secular education:*
   Foster, Josephine C., and Headley, Neith E., *Education in the Kindergarten*
   Leavitt, Jerome Edward, ed., *Nursery-Kindergarten Education*
   Sheehy, Emma D., *The Fives and Sixes Go to School*
   Wills, Clarice D., and Stegeman, William H., *Living in the Kindergarten*
4. *To study kindergarten work in the church:*
   Church and the Kindergarten Child — a portfolio, Evangelical and Reformed Church
   Learning Experiences for Young Children — a preschool program series, National Council of Churches
   Roorbach, Rosemary K., *Religion in the Kindergarten*
   Shields, Elizabeth McE., and Mallard, Dorothea G., *Guiding Kindergarten Children in the Church School*
5. *To better understand our faith:*
   Anderson, Bernhard W., *Rediscovering the Bible*

Henderlite, Rachel, *Call to Faith*

Howe, Reuel L., *Man's Need and God's Action*

Hunt, George L., *Rediscovering the Church*

Hunter, Archibald M., *The Work and Words of Jesus*

6. *Sources for equipment and materials:*

   Adair, Thelma, and McCort, Elizabeth, *How to Make Church School Equipment*

   Catalogue, Community Playthings, Rifton, N. Y.

   Catalogue, Creative Playthings, Inc., 5 University Place, New York 3, N. Y.

   Creating with Materials for Work and Play, Association for Childhood Education, International, 1200 Fifteenth Street, N.W., Washington 5, D.C.

AUDIO-VISUALS

It is wise to write for fuller descriptions of these audio-visuals or to see them before planning to use them.

Children's Emotions, 16mm. film, sound, 22 minutes. Approximate rental, black and white, $4.00. Available from McGraw-Hill Book Company, Inc., Text-Film Department, 330 West 42nd Street, New York 36, N. Y.

Four- and Five-Year-Olds in School, 16mm. film, sound, 37 minutes. Script. Approximate rental, black and white, $7.50. Available from New York University Film Library, 26 Washington Place, New York 3, N. Y.

The Kindergarten Child and the Church, filmstrip; 92 frames; 33⅓ r.p.m. record; script and guide. Produced by the National Council of Churches. Sale price, black and white, $10.00.

Principles of Development, 16mm. film, sound, 17 minutes. Approximate rental, black and white, $4.00. Available from McGraw-Hill Book Company, Inc., Text-Film Department, 330 West 42nd Street, New York 36, N. Y.

The Frustrating Fours and Fascinating Fives, 16mm. film, sound, 22 minutes. Approximate rental, black and white, $4.50. Available from McGraw-Hill Book Company, Inc., Text-Film Department, 330 West 42nd Street, New York 36, N. Y.